INVENTING
WESTERN
CIVILIZATION

INVENTING WESTERN CIVILIZATION

Thomas C. Patterson

MONTHLY REVIEW PRESS
NEW YORK

Library of Congress Cataloging-in-Publication Data

Patterson, Thomas Carl.
    Inventing western civilization / Thomas C. Patterson.
      p.   cm. — (Cornerstone books)
    Includes bibliographical references and index.
    ISBN 0-85345-960-6 (alk. Paper). — ISBN 0-84535-961-4 (pbk.)
    1. Civilization, Western.
I. Title.
II. Series: Cornerstone books (New York, N.Y.)
CB245.P339 1995   95-3435
909'.09821—dc20   CIP

Monthly Review Press
122 West 27th Street
New York, NY 10001

Manufactured in the United States of America
10 9 8 7 6 5 4 3

CONTENTS

ACKNOWLEDGMENTS

Anyone familiar with the literature on civilization and the topics surveyed in this book will immediately recognize the intellectual debt I owe to Stanley Diamond. I have also benefited in various ways from the constructive comments and observations of Ananth Aiyer, Niyi Akinnaso, Susan Porter Benson, David Brooks, Elizabeth Brumfiel, Carole Crumley, Christine Gailey, Sandra Harding, Susan Lowes, Joan Martin, Don Nonini, David Reichard, Mike Rowlands, Karen Brodkins Sacks, Karen Spalding, Jon Steinberg, and Ethan Young.

INVENTING CIVILIZATION

The word *civilization* evokes powerful images and understandings. We in the United States have been taught, from elementary school onward, that a few ancient peoples—like the Egyptians or Greeks—were "civilized" and that civilization achieved its highest level of development here and in other Western countries. Civilization, we are told, is beneficial, desirable—and definitely preferable to being uncivilized. The idea of civilization thus always implicitly involves a comparison: the existence of civilized people implies that there are uncivilized folk who are inferior because they are *not* civilized. Uncivilized peoples, for their part, have either been told that they can never become civilized or that they *should* become civilized as soon as possible; many of those who have tried or been forced to do so—such as the inhabitants of Bikini Atoll who were displaced from their homes so the United States could explode atom bombs in their lagoon after World War II—have suffered greatly as a result of the advance of civilization.

Civilization is an idea that we learned in school. Further, it is an elitist idea, one that is defined by creating hierarchies—of societies, of classes, of cultures, or of races. For the elites that coined the idea, civilizations are always class-stratified, state-based societies, and civilized peoples always belong to the those classes whose privileged existences are guaranteed by the institutions and practices of the state. Uncivilized peoples, in this view, do not belong to those classes, or else they live on the margins of civilization, where the ability of the state to control their lives is weak or episodic.

The word *civilization* is probably used more frequently in the media today than at any time since the years immediately following World War II. Media experts simultaneously extol the virtues of civilization and warn us of threats to its existence. They remind us again and again that it is good to be civilized. After all, civilization is marked by technological progress, greater productivity, and higher standards of living. Moreover, civilized people are polished and refined, wealthier and happier than their predecessors. But, the media experts warn, crime, violence, declining test scores in public schools, and the disintegration of "values" either threaten civilization, or else they are already signs of its decline.

For Newt Gingrich, the current speaker of the House of Representatives, the latter are evidence of a monumental crisis in American civilization. In fact, civilization is one of Gingrich's favorite topics. He uses the word in almost every speech or pronouncement. He does not mean civilization in any vague sense; he does not even mean Western civilization. He means *American* civilization. The United States is a civilization whose founding principles—personal strength, free enterprise, a spirit of invention and discovery, and the uniqueness of the American experience—have set it on a different trajectory from that of, for instance, Europe.[1]

Gingrich believes that the crisis in American civilization is in part the result of the failure of the institutions and programs that underpinned the Great Society programs of the mid-1960s. As he puts it, these "ruined the poor" and "created a culture of poverty and a culture

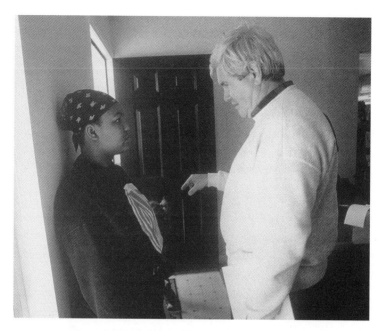

Newt Gingrich gives his views on welfare reform to a single mother in
Powder Springs, Georgia, 1995. [Bill Clark/Impact Visuals]

of violence which is destructive of this civilization."[2] For Gingrich,
these cultures of violence and poverty threaten the future of American
civilization because they embody habits and values that are the opposite of those needed if the new information-based civilization of the
twenty-first century is to unfold. He has put this very crudely: "It is
impossible to maintain civilization with twelve-year-olds having ba-
bies, fifteen-year-olds killing each other, seventeen-year-olds dying of
AIDS, and with eighteen-year-olds ending up with diplomas they can
barely read."[3]

Gingrich also believes that American civilization is threatened by
the cultural diversity found in the United States in the late twentieth
century. He believes that this diversity was in part as a result of massive

in-migration since the 1960s, as well as the civil rights movement, which demanded equal treatment and rights, and affirmative action programs, which provided a few economic opportunities to women and minorities. Gingrich believes that the state must control this diversity in order to preserve what is quintessentially American:

> For America to survive as a civilization, English has to be our common language…. If we allow the multicultural model of a multilingual America to become dominant, this society will disintegrate.[4]

For Gingrich and those who think as he does, the Spanish-speaking enclaves in metropolitan Miami and Los Angeles, French-speaking neighborhoods in small New England towns like Waterville, Maine, or Haitian Creole-speaking neighborhoods in Brooklyn, all threaten American civilization by their very existence.

Let us stop for a moment to consider precisely what Gingrich means when he uses the word civilization. For one thing, in a civilized society, the state should enact legislation to achieve certain goals. One goal should be to ensure technological progress at a steadily accelerating pace, since the key to the future of American civilization is the development of a high-tech information economy. Thus, the government, in its role as consumer of high-tech goods, should stimulate technological innovation, which will then trickle down to broader markets.

The advanced, high-tech civilization that Gingrich envisages is also a society rooted in inequalities of various kinds. For instance, he wants the state to pass laws that redistribute income upward. And since civilization involves culture and values, the state should also pass laws that promote certain kinds of values and behavior. For example, it should require that only English be spoken in public places. Practices that aid women or members of minority groups should either be placed under the control of men, restricted, or criminalized. Civilized people, according to Gingrich, are those who cultivate the beliefs, values, and goals that encourage "refined" behavior. Those who will not or cannot subscribe to such standards are by definition the barbarians, or the underclasses, whose existence is a threat to civilization.

Gingrich's fears are echoed by Roger Kimball's commentary a few years ago on the dangers of multiculturalism—a perspective which recognizes that different communities have different cultural practices and values. Kimball wrote:

> The choice facing us today is not between a "repressive" Western culture and a multicultural paradise, but between culture and barbarism. Civilization is not a gift, it is an achievement—a fragile achievement that needs constantly to be shored up and defended from besiegers inside and out.[5]

Gingrich's claims about the loss of standards are also buttressed by the arguments of Richard Herrnstein and Charles Murray, the authors of *The Bell Curve: Intelligence and Class Structure in American Life* (1994), even though they build on a different logic. Herrnstein and Murray assert that the growing income differential between high school and college graduates indicates that cognitive ability and, by extension, the ability to recognize these "objective standards" are more commonly found among highly educated individuals with high socioeconomic status, most of whom are white. In their view, the IQ gap between whites and Asians, on the one hand, and blacks, on the other, is largely immutable, even though it closes in the higher socioeconomic status groups.[6] The reason for this, they suggest, is that the old social Darwinist and eugenics arguments were basically correct: that about 60 percent of human intelligence is inherited—even though the genes for cognitive ability still have not been found after a well-funded, century-long search. They further argue that the picture has been complicated by affirmative action programs, and suggest that planners take these hereditary racial differences in cognitive ability into account and devise policies which will allow everyone to be a "morally autonomous human being."[7]

Gingrich's views about civilization also resonate with those of Samuel Huntington, the Harvard political scientist whose policy research over the years has supported large budgets for the Pentagon. In the mid-1970s, Huntington gained a certain notoriety when he suggested that too much democracy was dangerous, and that states should be led by properly educated elites.[8] In his view, there are seven or eight competing civilizations in the world today: Western, Confucian, Japanese, Islamic, Hindu, Slavic-Orthodox, Latin American, and possibly African. The real danger results from the fact that they are locked in a potentially life-and-death struggle, a clash of civilizations. While the major struggles from the 1890s through the end of the cold war were conflicts within Western civilization, the clash looming on the horizon is a struggle between Western civilization and the non-Western world, parts of which are also civilized.

Civilizations, for Huntington, are cultural entities that will become increasingly important in current and future conflicts. A civilization is

> the highest cultural grouping of a people and the broadest level of cultural identity people have short of that which distinguishes humans from other species. It is defined both by objective elements, such as language, history, religion, customs, institutions, and by the subjective self-identification of people. People have levels of identity: a resident of Rome may define himself as a Roman, an Italian, a Catholic, a Christian, a European, a Westerner. The civilization to which he belongs is the broadest level of identification with which he intensely identifies.[9]

Huntington believes that Western civilization is "the universal civilization," while the others are still regional. Since he defines civilization on the basis of cultural differences, his list reflects real differences of language, culture, and tradition, and, most importantly, religion, which in his view is really the most important feature distinguishing one civilization from another. As a result, the people of different civilizations have different views about the relations between God and man, the individual and the group, the citizen and the state, parents and children, husband and wife, as well as differing views of the relative importance of rights and responsibilities, liberty and authority, equality and hierarchy. These differences are the product of centuries. They will not soon disappear.[10]

While the trappings of Western civilization have been adopted throughout the world at a superficial level, its more basic concepts, which are fundamentally different from those of other civilizations, have not.

Western ideas of individualism, liberalism, constitutionalism, human rights, equality, liberty, the rule of law, democracy, free markets, the separation of church and state, often have little resonance in Islamic, Confucian, Japanese, Hindu, Buddhist or Orthodox cultures.[11]

The interactions between diverse peoples have intensified as the world has become smaller; this has increased everyone's awareness of both the differences between civilizations and the commonalities within them. Huntington claims this increased familiarity has bred contempt and rekindled centuries-old animosities. He also claims that increased civilizational consciousness in the former colonies has led to a decline in Western influence, as the Western-educated elites of these countries seek their own ancient roots and as the masses increasingly reject Western cultural styles and commodities.

Since the cultural forms of the civilizations underpinning the former colonies are so persistent, they are much less easily changed than the economic characteristics these countries acquired in recent times. Consequently, civilizational consciousness is particularly important during this period of economic transformation, because it provides the cultural foundations for the emergence of new economic regions. In his view, the common culture shared by Taiwan, the People's Republic of China, Hong Kong, Singapore, and the overseas Chinese has facilitated the rapid expansion of economic interconnections.[12]

The greatest problems, according to Huntington, exist in multicultural or multicivilizational countries—like Mexico and the successor states that emerged after the disintegration of the USSR and Yugoslavia. These "torn" countries were composed of large numbers of peoples from different civilizations: that is, their citizens spoke different languages and practiced different religions. They were, Huntington argues, unstable mosaics of Western, Slavic-Orthodox, and Islamic civilizations held together by communism—an imported Western ideology. When that ideology was discredited in the waning years of the cold war, they fell apart, and the different civilizations were able to reassert their identities and claim political autonomy. Implicitly, those countries which are torn by inter-civilizational rivalries point to the real dangers of multiculturalism: class struggle and civil war.

In Huntington's view, the residents of a country can voluntarily redefine their civilizational identities. Three conditions are necessary for this to happen:

> First, its political and economic elites have to be generally supportive of and enthusiastic about this move. Second, its public has to be willing to acquiesce in the redefinition. Third, the dominant groups in the recipient civilization have to be willing to embrace the convert.[13]

It is clear, however, that not all of the torn countries will redefine their identities as Western and adopt a value system which proclaims the political hegemony of the United States and Western Europe. To become Western means that they might, in fact, find themselves in direct competition with the West rather than attached to them in some subordinate role. Thus, in Huntington's view,

> The obstacles to non-Western countries joining the West vary considerably. They are least for Latin American and Eastern European countries. They are greater for the Orthodox countries of the former Soviet Union. They

are still greater for Muslim, Confucian, Hindu, and Buddhist societies. Japan has established a unique position.... [I]t is in the West in some respects but clearly not of the West in important dimensions.[14]

While the Western countries and Russia were reducing their military power, claims Huntington, a number of states—China, North Korea, Iraq, Iran, Libya, and Algeria—expanded their military capabilities by importing arms from various Western and non-Western sources or by developing their own arms industries. These non-Western "weapons states" threaten both the existing balance of forces and the West's post-cold war objective to prevent the spread of arms that would threaten its hegemony. The Confucian-Islamic connection which now challenges Western interests and power is defined largely in civilizational terms. Huntington's remedy, like that of the modernization theorists in the 1950s and 1960s, is to maintain the military superiority of the West, especially in East and Southwest Asia;

to exploit differences and conflicts among Confucian and Islamic states; to support in other civilizations groups sympathetic to Western values and interests; to strengthen international institutions that reflect and legitimate Western interests and values and to promote the involvement of non-Western states in those institutions.[15]

To achieve these goals, the West must recognize that, for the foreseeable future, the world will be one in which different civilizations coexist. It must also

develop a more profound understanding of the basic religious and philosophical assumptions underlying those civilizations and the ways in which people in those civilizations see their interests. It will require an effort to identify elements of commonality between Western and other civilizations.[16]

Huntington's discussion captures other dimensions of the idea of civilization. Civilizations involve the construction of identity under particular historical and social circumstances. They often cross the boundaries of modern states, so that Western civilization, for example, is found both in the United States and the countries of Western Europe. Some states, like Mexico or the former USSR, are multicultural or multi-civilizational but not Western, and their social fabrics are fragile because of the potential for conflict erupting among the various constituents.

Huntington also points to the relation between civilization and the class structure of a particular state. The political and economic elites—that is, the ruling class—provide the impetus for changing or redefining civilizational identity. Once they have voluntarily decided to change, they must then attempt to convince the subordinated classes and communities of the wisdom of their views before they can set a new worldview in place. In his view, civilizational change is always a top-down process initiated by the elite.

The United States and the countries of Western Europe are not the only states reviving the idea of civilization. Civil society, a closely related idea, is now widely discussed in the former USSR and Eastern bloc countries.[17] The reason for the renewed popularity of these concepts, I believe, is that they are important and necessary parts of the ideological baggage linked to processes of class and state formation. Since these processes are currently unfolding on an almost global scale, intellectuals are using civilization and related concepts to invent different versions of the same story, which is organized around the idea that hierarchy and inequality are not only necessary but natural.

Each class-stratified, state-based society invents its own particular vision of civilization. What is striking are the remarkable similarities of the portraits that have been painted over time. For instance, Chinese intellectuals of the late third century b.c. defined the social order of the Han world and civilization in terms of a five-zone theory. In their view, the world was divided into five concentric rings that were hierarchically organized. At the center of the civilized world was the royal domain, and the king extracted tribute on a daily basis from its residents. The lords resided in the next zone, and the king received tribute on a monthly basis. Further away was pacified zone, whose inhabitants provided him with tribute every three months. Still further away from the center were the frontier lands inhabited by the tamed or controlled barbarians who gave tribute once a year. Finally, there were the wild lands, beyond the frontiers of Chinese civilization, that were occupied by wild barbarians who perhaps paid tribute once in a lifetime.[18]

The Inca rulers of fifteenth-century Peru also viewed themselves as an island of civilization in a sea of barbarians. Unlike the Han emperors, the Inca rulers claimed that they were created separately from the rest of humanity, and that, by virtue of their direct descent from the sun deity, they were divinely ordained to rule their kin and neighbors. It was their duty to bring peace, justice, and civilization to the Andean peoples, especially to the savages who lived on the periphery of the Inca state. In return for these gifts, the Incas demanded that subject populations make tribute payments that would be collected annually through local intermediaries; if they threatened to withhold tribute destined for the Inca royal families or the state, the Incas threatened to respond with force: to disperse their members, seize their herds, and even destroy their crops.[19]

THE BOOK AND ITS ORGANIZATION

Some commentators believe that people acquire civilization when they transform nature through hard work and, in the process, better themselves and their circumstances. Others see it as inherited, part of a historical tradition that is passed by the elites from one generation to the next. For some it is rooted in social relations; for others, it is an expression of biological superiority.

Writers who extol the virtues of civilization usually invoke two additional concepts to bolster their views. One is *nature* and the other

An illustration from a 1,200-page letter sent to the King
of Spain in 1615 by Felipe Guaman Poma, a native Indian of Peru.
The letter attacked the behavior of the Peruvian colonial state toward
the Andean peoples. Here he depicts the maltreatment of black slaves
by members of the colonial elite.

is *the uncivilized*—whom they usually define as those groups that follow their natural instincts, unfettered by the civilized virtues of law and order. Together, the two concepts function to create the shadow or mirror image of civilization. Whereas civilization consists of the refined institutions, moral values, and cultures of states and their elites, nature is the essential (natural) condition from which they emerged and to which they are therefore opposed. Uncivilized peoples represent the primary (primitive) or unrefined stages of the human condition which, depending on how the civilized (ruling) classes portray their own history, they either avoided altogether or passed through at an earlier time.

We shall see in the chapters that follow that civilized people are obsessed with their uncivilized kin and neighbors—those they call *savages, barbarians,* or the "masses" who lack their polish, refinement, and sophistication; who reside beyond their borders; and who, in times of massive migration, have moved en masse into their midst. This obsession with the uncivilized peoples is exacerbated in states, like the liberal democracies of modern times, where parts of the ruling class itself come from among the less civilized, less cultured lower classes and subject populations, from foreigners, and from recent immigrants.[20]

An essential feature of civilization, therefore, is social stratification—that is, a set of hierarchical relations through which contempt for and fear of the "other" (among other sentiments) are expressed. These sentiments affect both rulers and subjects, although they are experienced in different ways.[21] The ruling classes, which portray themselves as the mainstay of civilization, claim that their views are superior to those of their less civilized subjects, as well as to the beliefs and practices of those uncivilized communities over which they have little or no control. Their fears ultimately rest on their distrust of the uncivilized masses. They fear the day when their subjects will refuse to comply with their demands, when their threats and coercion will be resisted, and when their legitimacy will be challenged.

The rage of the uncivilized classes is the result of their exploitation. Their fears derive from the realization that the exactions of the state may become so onerous that their members will no longer be able to provide for themselves and their families. The rise of civilization therefore ultimately is accompanied by the construction of social classes, the subordination of women, and the creation of "others" who are distinguished by appearances, behaviors, or essences that are attributed to them. Thus class, sexism, and racism are as integral to civilized society as inequality and alienation; they are also integral features of all descriptions of civilization.

Civilization is not a thing: it is an idea, a concept, a way of organizing reality. This book will focus on the development of only one idea of civilization, Western civilization, which was first constructed in Renaissance Europe and then refined by Enlightenment social commentators in northern Europe in the eighteenth century. Through the decades, it has been argued that Western civilization began in Greece and Rome, passed to northern Europe during the age of overseas expansion and industrialization, and was finally brought to the United States, where it flourished, matured, and produced its greatest achievements in the nineteenth and twentieth centuries. While the elite intellectuals who crafted the idea of Western civilization admitted that there were other civilizations—the Semitic civilization of North Africa and the Middle East, the civilizations of China and Japan, the Maya and Inca high cultures of Central and South America—they believed that none had reached the level of achievement attained by Rome and Greece and the societies that descended from that tradition.[22]

This book is about civilization, which means that it is about social and cultural hierarchies and inequality. It is also about the consequences of having been trained to look at the world through the eyes of the elite. Since the boosters of civilization have always been inherently antidemocratic, they have been opposed to the existence of classless societies and to visions of truly egalitarian social relations. Like the barbarians at the gates of Rome, even the idea that societies without social classes and the state might exist challenges the very foundations of the privileged lifestyles of the civilized classes.

I have organized the book to explore the idea of civilization and its interplay with other ideas—such as culture, backwardness, progress, modernity, history, tradition, and nature—that are also deployed to legitimate social hierarchy. The reasons for this approach will hopefully become apparent as the text unfolds.

Chapter 2 deals with one side of an argument about civilization. It presents the views of intellectuals who celebrated civilization and deployed the idea beginning with the colonial ventures of the sixteenth century. Their influence derived from their relation to ruling classes. In their hands, civilization became a theory of history, describing the change from a primitive—that is, a primary or original—condition to a more advanced one by means of moral, intellectual, and social progress. This allowed them to view their own societies as more advanced than those of native peoples in the colonies or of Greece and Rome. This view was fueled by the rise of capitalism, the scientific and industrial revolutions, the appearance of modern states, and the Enlightenment. They coined the word "civilization" in the 1760s to describe the development of social conditions created by capitalism and the formation of an educated elite. From 1800 onwards, the boosters of civilization compared theirs with other kinds of societies and sought to explain the forces that underpinned its development.

Chapter 3 presents the other side of the argument about civilization. From the sixteenth century onwards, critics developed various unflattering assessments of the rise of Western civilization. They criticized the way the civilized states of Western Europe dealt with their colonial subjects. They also criticized the effects that the rise of civilization had on their own societies in Western Europe, such as increased inequality, the steadily increasing immiseration of the masses, and the crystal-lization of an elite culture. The chapter examines critiques with different theoretical underpinnings: radical, romantic, liberal, nationalist, and cultural.

Chapter 4 looks at the mirror images of civilization—the barbarians and other uncivilized peoples invented or recycled by the mostly male agents of civilization. They were foreigners that dwelled on the fringes of the civilized world, and they were the women and subordinated classes of civilization itself. In eras of massive migration, like today, these uncivilized peoples reside increasingly in the civilized world. In ancient Athens, barbarians were the foreigners who provided Greek dramatists with alternatives to Athenian culture. The diversity of uncivilized peoples increased with overseas expansion, the formation of settler colonies, the growth of the slave trade, and the rise of capitalism. Culture, gender, class, and race (a new idea of the late seventeenth century) became bases for defining communities and individuals as the noncivilized other. Uncivilized peoples are always assigned to subordinate positions in the social hierarchies associated with civilization. Since they provide an alternative to civilization itself, their continued existence and even memories of their existence are threatening to civilized society.

Chapter 5 presents the views of the peoples who were subordinated and marginalized as they were incorporated into the American version of Western civilization. The men and women who constituted these groups had refreshingly clear understandings of the exploitative and oppressive conditions in which they lived. They challenged the descriptive categories of the uncivilized race, class, gender, or person invented by the boosters of civilization. Their views call into question the utility of the unqualified or uncritical idea of civilization. They also force us to think about whose interests are served when we continue to use the idea of civilization uncritically or nondialectically.

In sum, this book is concerned with the idea of civilization and how people have talked about civilized peoples and their uncivilized neighbors. It examines the shifting social and political conditions in which civilization is produced and deployed, and how in various ways civilization has structured discourses about power while creating and perpetuating heritages and graphic images of past and contemporary peoples. This book challenges the view implicit in the idea of *civilization itself* that males, usually white, are the dominant actors and all others are passive.

CIVILIZATION AND ITS BOOSTERS

The idea of *civilization* was a major part of the ideology that accompanied and buttressed the rise of the modern European state.[1] The modern state emerged within the crisis of feudalism—a crisis that was characterized by declining incomes among the ruling class, even in periods of economic expansion.[2] The appearance of the modern state began during the Renaissance and gained momentum after enormous quantities of plunder began to arrive from the Americas in the 1500s. By that time, the European states already had diverse forms of government: absolutist monarchies in Spain, France, and England; states dominated by clerical corporations in the Holy Roman Empire—that is, parts of what is now Germany and central Italy; and republics with parliamentary assemblies in what is now northern Italy and Switzerland.

The formation of modern states was also connected with the emergence of social classes that marked new relationships between monarchs, nobles, and their subjects. In feudal regimes, the nobility derived its livelihood from land acquired through war, and from the labor and goods they extracted from their subjects; they were also the judicial authority in their own domain. During the Renaissance, the princes and kings began to hire literate men—intellectuals—to help them manage their estates and cash in on the benefits of centralizing state government. In the absolutist monarchies that appeared in the early sixteenth century, the monarchs treated the state as a personal enterprise, a potentially lucrative extension of their own households, even though they often had to share this wealth with others.

By the early 1500s, the rulers of Spain, France, and England had begun to consolidate their political power in order to acquire revenues so that they could conduct wars, diplomacy, trade, and colonization. They sold political offices to literate nobles, burghers, and churchmen, and they demanded monetary payment for the taxes levied directly on town-dwellers and farmers. This was the beginning of a state bureaucracy, whose officials were concerned mainly with tax-collecting and census-taking. The new administrators also profited from their offices, and the nobles who had purchased offices received cash revenues instead of feudal tribute payments in labor and kind.

State intervention was the most important feature of the economic policies of this period. The newly centralized states were able to promote the development of internal markets, to encourage the export of commodities, and to profit from both. Many states—notably Spain, Portugal, France, England, and Holland—sponsored overseas colonial enterprises that created markets for their merchants and manufacturers and provided revenues for their rulers. They also prohibited the export of gold bullion, which was viewed as the main source of wealth.

Before long, the rulers of the new states hired university-trained lawyers to explore and specify the nature of the new social relationships that were developing as a result of these changes. These men had studied Roman law, which provided a model for drawing distinctions between citizens and subjects, describing their relation to the state, and regulating their economic activities and relations with one another. It was these officials who first began to elaborate the idea of civilization.[3] In the 1560s, French jurists such as Jean Bodin and Loys Le Roy, the offspring of wealthy merchant families whose fame and fortune rested on their close ties to the king, began to set the standard. They used the words *civilité* and *civilisé* to describe peoples, like themselves, who were governed according to certain political forms, whose arts and letters exhibited a certain degree of sophistication, and whose manners and morality were considered superior to those of other members of their own societies or the members of other societies. They did not consider the peasants in their own societies to be urbane, courteous, civil, or literate. The same was believed to be true of indigenous peoples who lived in the wilderness of the new colonies. From the eleventh century onward, these "uncivilized" folks were often described as "rustics"—that is, countrymen who, by virtue of their lowly place in society, were deemed stupid, coarse, and ill-mannered.[4]

The Crown intellectuals, steeped as they were in studies of ancient Roman law, were familiar with the French words' Latin roots in the words *civilis*, *civis*, and their cognates. In their historical context, the Latin words conveyed a set of interconnected meanings, including: the fellowship of citizens; the law as enforced on and adhered to by citizens; behavior as an ordinary person or citizen; the legal domain as opposed to the military; politics; association with state administration; and an organized community to which one belongs as a citizen of a state. Civilization, in other words, was state-based, class-stratified, and ruled by law; its literate fraction either belonged to the ruling class or held important positions in the state apparatus.

OVERSEAS EXPANSION

The idea of civilization was forged in the context of European overseas colonial expansion into Africa, Asia, the Americas, and Ireland. It was used by the elites of the states that launched these ventures to distinguish themselves from the peoples they encountered. As they moved overseas, the Europeans used customary categories of the time, such as *wild men, heathens, infidels, pagans, savages,* and *barbarians,* to describe the peoples they met who lacked writing, organized governments, class structures, or permanent places of residence.

England's conquest and colonization of Ireland in the 1570s, for instance, provided a model for its subsequent colonial ventures in North America. The goal of Sir Thomas Smith, secretary of state and a student of Spanish imperialism in the Americas, was to transform Ireland into a colony in order to exploit Irish labor and make the Irish permanently dependent on the English settlers. This necessitated the subjugation of the Irish lords who ruled most of the island.

The explicit goal of Smith's colonial venture was therefore to forge and maintain a social hierarchy, with the English settlers at the top of the ladder and the Irish below. He planned to do this by subjugating the Irish economically, politically, and socially:

> Every Irishman shall be forbidden to wear English apparel or weapon upon pain of death. That no Irishman, born of the Irish race and brought up Irish, shall purchase land, bear office, be chosen of any jury, or admitted witness in any real or personal action, not be bound apprentice to any art or science that may endamage the queen majesty's subjects.[5]

To justify these acts of brutality and subjugation, Smith invoked the concept of civilization. To Smith, only the English, like the Romans of classical antiquity, could bring the rule of law, peace, and civility to the colony. The inhabitants of Ireland were "a wicked, barbarous and uncivil people, some Scottish and some wild Irish."[6] In fact, he believed that the Irish could never be civilized: they were nomads who followed their herds and were therefore barbarians—only sedentary peoples could be civilized. Furthermore, in a milieu shaped by the religious wars of the Reformation, Smith viewed the Irish as little better than pagans or infidels, even though they professed to be Catholics.

At about this same time, a Jesuit missionary in Peru named José de Acosta was exploring the relationship between civilized peoples, barbarians, and savages in the Americas. Acosta had arrived in Peru in 1572. He believed that Christian teaching had done little to eradicate the idolatrous pagan beliefs and practices of the Andean peoples. Indeed, Quechua, the indigenous language, did not even have a vocabulary that could convey the subtleties of Christianity. In *The Nature of the New World*, written in the late 1570s, Acosta constructed a categorization of non-Christian societies based on the kinds of idolatry their members practiced and on the methods that would lead to their conversion. For instance, there were non-Christian monarchies, like China and Japan, that had writing and governments; their members could be converted to Christianity through peaceful teaching. Then there were illiterate barbarians, like the Incas and Aztecs, who had governments and fixed places of residence but whose members lacked the intelligence and reasoning ability of the ancient Greeks and Romans; converting them would require a strong Christian ruler who would enforce their adherence to the Christian religion. Finally, there were savages—like the peoples of the Amazon basin—who lacked laws, government, and permanent settlements; their conversion could only be accomplished by force and required the collaboration of soldiers and missionaries.[7]

The importance of Acosta's book was not so much in his categorization of uncivilized peoples, but rather in the position he ultimately held. He was the King of Spain's representative to the Pope. By virtue of this position, as well as his vast experience in the Americas, Acosta was the acknowledged and most widely read authority on American Indian cultures from the 1580s to 1781. His views were accepted as fact by most writers concerned with native peoples and colonial affairs for nearly two centuries.

THE IDEA OF PROGRESS

Most sixteenth-century writers did not believe that typologies such as these represented a historical development or genealogical sequence that developed over time. Instead, they continued to believe one of two competing theories: that humanity had *degenerated* from a past golden age; or that, based on the prophecies in the Book of Daniel, history was divided into four periods corresponding to the Babylonian, Persian, Macedonian, and Roman empires, the last of which would survive until Judgment Day. However, Le Roy, the advisor to the French king, was familiar with Plato's claim that the first human beings were naked forest dwellers and drew what was to him an obvious inference: the ancient inhabitants of Europe had to have been as rude and uncivilized as the contemporary forest-dwelling savages that the Portuguese and Spaniards had discovered in Africa and the Americas. In *Of the Origin, Antiquity, Progress, Excellence, and Utility of the Political Art* (1568), Le Roy used the verb *civiliser* to describe the process by which change from a primitive, natural condition to a more advanced one was effected by means of moral, intellectual, and social progress. For Le Roy and other members of court intelligentsia, life in the present was obviously superior to life in the past; change was assumed to be cumulative, directional, and desirable.[8] Today the belief that the societies of modern Europe are more advanced than their predecessors—that there is such a thing as *progress*—is so embedded in our thinking that it seems self-evident; but at the time it was new.

Jean Bodin, political theorist and advisor to the French king, used this belief in progress to reinterpret the course of human history. In *The Six Books of the Republic* (1577), he rejected the two competing theories and argued that human history was divided into *three* periods, each more civilized than the last. Each period was dominated by the peoples of a particular geographical area. The Oriental peoples—the Babylonians, Persians, and Egyptians—dominated the first two millennia because of their innovations in religion, philosophy, and mathematics, and their ability to unravel the secrets of nature. The Mediterranean peoples—the Greeks and Romans—reigned for the next two millennia because of their practical knowledge, gifted statesmanship, and politics. Finally, the Northern nations came to the fore because of their skill in warfare and their mechanical inventions. For Bodin, then, the shifting center of human history was the result of natural conditions acting on peoples with different capabilities and weaknesses.[9]

Bodin and other authors of universal histories laid the foundations for the theory of historical development of Western civilization that dominates today: Civilization began in the Holy Land, passed to Greece and Rome, and then reached its highest levels in the nations of northern Europe (and, later, the United States). In this view, the human condition improved slowly but steadily from one period to the next. The peoples of northern Europe (modern society) extended the achievements and knowledge of ancient authorities through observation and experience, rather than rigid adherence to their views. They also capitalized on inventions, like the compass, that enabled them to extend their horizons far beyond those of the ancient Babylonians or Romans; this and other inventions underwrote advances in commerce and laid the foundations for an ever-expanding world whose nations were linked together by business and trade rather than faith.[10]

REASON, SCIENCE, AND THE BEGINNINGS OF MODERNITY

The idea of progress was extended by two Crown intellectuals, one French and one English, during the Thirty Years War (1618-1648) and the civil wars that followed in its wake. Francis Bacon and René Descartes believed that *reason* was a uniquely human attribute that differentiated people from animals and nature, both of which were actually mindless mechanisms that could be described mathematically. In their view, if reason were applied systematically, then custom and superstition could be eliminated, nature conquered, and social institutions improved. Reason was an abstract skill that did not depend on particular bodies of concrete subject matter. It was an instrument that any human being—properly schooled in the scientific method, of course—could apply.

Given the existing class structure and limited access to education, Bacon and Descartes believed that reason was the domain of elite men, who would ultimately usher in a new age in human history, an era in which rationality would swamp tradition.

Bacon, the one-time clerk of the infamous Star Chamber, the ruthlessly inquisitorial royal court, argued that the application of reason would solve the legal and political problems confronting statesmen. It would also make science a royal enterprise that would profit from the conquest of nature. Bacon believed in an imperial monarchy and felt that science would provide the monarch with revenues and thereby strengthen the imperial state. In *Novum Organum* (1620), he made two proposals toward this end. The first was a set of procedures, now called the scientific method, which resembled a judge and jury sifting through piles of information to establish the facts of a particular case. The second was the creation of a set of state institutions that would involve large numbers of individuals, some of whom would be involved in the systematic collection of information and others of whom, properly educated in the scientific method, would create facts and interpret their significance.[11]

Descartes argued for the importance of reason in a slightly different way. In *Discourse on Method* (1637) he noted that half-savages began to behave rationally when they made laws to regulate crimes and quarrels. It was at this point that they became *civilized;* in other words, the application of reason was a civilizing process. He then argued that civilized (or modern) societies were both rationally organized and superior to their less rational predecessors and contemporaries. Their members applied reason to nurture change and progress in contrast to the savages and barbarians of static, backward societies.[12]

The growth of *reason*, for Bacon and Descartes, was the motor for progress. It distinguished the modern nations of northern Europe from their predecessors and from their savage contemporaries. Reason freed people from the restraints of tradition. It was the increased importance of reason in the affairs of the civilized peoples, they believed, that underwrote overseas expansion and technological innovation such as advances in printing, military ordnance, and navigational instruments. The growth of reason, i.e., the increased rationality of civilized people, would facilitate the conquest of nature, and this in turn would unleash rapid, beneficial, and profitable change. Viewing the growth of reason as the engine of progress meant that the future offered unlimited opportunities to civilized societies.

Seventeenth-century Crown servants and intellectuals carried this view to its logical conclusion: rationality untainted by human passions, ethics, or historical considerations was the hallmark of the modern civilization. Such modernity was a goal that should be pursued. As this view became politically dominant, the scientific procedures and models developed in physics or astronomy were employed to discover causal relations in others fields of inquiry, including the study of human society. The advocates of this mechanical worldview increasingly portrayed society as a machine that resembled a gigantic clock. By removing society from its historical context, they stripped away its content. As human society became an abstraction devoid of context and content, discussions of civil society, the state, and the civilized person were also framed in increasingly abstract terms.[13]

CIVILITY, CIVIL SOCIETY, AND THE STATE

In the 1600s, government officials and the intellectuals they employed linked the ideas of civility and civil society to the myth of government.[14] Theirs was an ideological project that served to legitimatize the kinds of states that were appearing in Western Europe. Civil society, in their view, could only flourish when and where there was government. This meant that the promulgation of laws to regulate crime and quarrels was, as Descartes has proposed, the essence of the civilizing process. Descartes and his contemporaries believed that without government even civilized peoples would revert to savagery. The logical conclusion was that European superiority existed precisely because of government and a social milieu that promoted development of the arts and sciences, and that without government, the motor of progress would stop and even be reversed.

State intellectuals in England, most notably Thomas Hobbes and John Locke, used a logical (not historical) reconstruction of the state of nature in order to describe the relationships between government, law, and civil society. In *Leviathan* (1651), Hobbes portrayed the natural condition of humanity as one of war, where life was solitary, brutal, and short. In this state of nature, human beings were separate individuals driven solely by the need to satisfy their physical and emotional appetites. The only way out of this deplorable condition (which he thought resembled that of American Indian societies) was to establish peace. And this could only be accomplished if individuals were conquered or ceded power to a sovereign who, in return, would ensure peace, justice, and proper behavior. In Hobbes's view, civil society was formed by the constitution of a government, which provided laws and prescribed forms of behavior appropriate to its citizens. Civil society then created the conditions and demands required for the development of industry, the arts, and knowledge.[15]

Locke provided an alternative view of the beginnings of civil society and the state in his *Second Treatise of Government* (1690). He believed that the process of accumulating property began in the state of nature, that the desire to accumulate was part of human nature, and that individuals who failed to do so were not acting rationally. The purpose of political society—i.e., the state—was to maintain men's natural right to life, liberty, and the property they had already accumulated. Thus Locke, unlike Hobbes, believed society had existed before men agreed to transfer to government the right to enforce law and order and to protect against aggression. If men were to take advantage of citizenship—which conferred responsibilities, rights, and powers onto citizens—they had to have leisure and education. In this view, civil society preserved the traditions of political society. It was the custodian of the manners and knowledge appropriate for citizens, who had to understand and respect the law and develop a sense of shared identity in order to enact legislation that would allow them to further their own interests—which were, of course, life, liberty, and the pursuit of property (or happiness, according to the signatories of the Declaration of Independence).[16]

For state officials and their intellectual employees, it was very important how an individual conducted himself in the company of others. This was the essence of civility. Civility prescribed the rules of behavior that defined a good citizen and specified the terms of participation in the inner circles of power. As a result, Locke paid considerable attention to education and to how the ideals of virtue, industry, and reputation were to be transmitted to the younger members of the upper classes in order to equip them for life in polite society. But the guidelines he formulated were to shape interpersonal relations among citizens, not those of classes or peoples outside the inner circles of power.[17]

POLITICAL ECONOMY, MORAL PHILOSOPHY, AND ENLIGHTENMENT

Many sixteenth-and seventeenth-century philosophers argued that the state was essential for the maintenance of social order, which, in turn, allowed civility and reason to flourish. The way intellectuals described the origins of civil society and its relation to the state began to change in the early 1700s. This was especially true in Scotland, which was undergoing massive social change. Before union with England in 1707, the peoples of the Highlands were organized into clans, whose members were related by kinship and whose households lived largely by farming, fishing, and hunting. Since they were economically self-sufficient and produced the goods they needed, they were not forced to purchase necessities in the marketplace. However, this society began to crumble after the union, as clan leaders began to sell their cattle and turn their croplands into pasture, displacing their kin and neighbors in the process. In order to survive, the newly dispossessed were forced to collect and sell kelp or to seek wage work in the new textile factories. The old way of life was rapidly being replaced by a society based on commerce and industry.

Scottish officials and intellectuals employed by the state, such as David Hume, James Steuart, and Adam Smith, attempted to explain these changes in terms that separated economics from politics. Hume, for instance, regarded the state as a necessary element of society, regulating economic relations between men by enforcing the principles of justice—which he understood to be the protection of property, trade, and contracts. However, he questioned the wisdom of state policies—

like tariffs, embargoes, and regulations to create a favorable balance of trade—that interfered with international commerce, which he saw as the major way of increasing the country's wealth and as the foundation of economic progress. He supported the development of manufacture and commerce, because they would stimulate agricultural production, expand consumption, promote intellectual and cultural refinement, and enhance the power of the state itself.[18]

James Steuart, Hume's contemporary, argued that the state rather than the market would be the source of economic progress. Since poor people, from Steuart's point of view, were incapable of making decisions for themselves, the state should underwrite the accumulation of wealth and maintain the existing social hierarchy. He suggested how this might be accomplished:

> [N]othing is impossible to an able statesman. When a people can be engaged to murder their wives and children, and to burn themselves, rather than submit to a foreign enemy; when they can be brought to give their most precious effects, their ornaments of gold and silver, for the support of the common cause; ... I think I may say, that by properly conducting and managing the spirit of a people, nothing is impossible to be accomplished.[19]

Adam Smith, like many of his contemporaries in Scotland, constructed a historical narrative that would explain the rise of commercial society. In his view, social progress was a natural, law-driven process that was tied to changes in the mode of subsistence production. The first societies, Smith argued, were composed of small numbers of individuals who provisioned themselves by hunting and foraging. As their numbers increased, they domesticated animals and became herders. As their numbers increased further, those communities that occupied favorable environments in temperate areas turned to agriculture. This was followed by a significantly increased division of labor as artisans ceased to produce their own food and settled in towns to pursue their crafts and to barter goods or exchange them for money. The endpoint of this process was the kind of commercial and civil society that was then emerging in many European countries.[20]

For Smith, human society was organized like a factory, and the increasing division of labor characteristic of commercial society in Europe had arisen because of a human propensity to barter and exchange. This inclination led to the elaboration of the division of labor and to changes in the mode of production, which accompanied the rise of commercial society.

Commercial society was the product of a complex relationship between politics and economics. Smith's historical inquiries led him to believe that the "hidden hand of the market"—mankind's continual effort to create an increasingly dense web of social relations through exchange—operated only when exchange was possible and when it was as free as possible from state control. However, the state was required to maintain social order and provide stability needed for the extension of the division of labor, the accumulation of capital, and the protection of the diverse forms of property ownership that arose in commercial societies. In a class-stratified society, those who were so protected were, of course, members of the most fortunate class. And as government increasingly became the domain of that class, it not only became less responsive to the sentiments of the other classes, but more and more became an instrument for oppressing them.[21]

While Smith recognized the contradictions surrounding the role of the state in commercial society, he ultimately opted for a form of government that would ensure social order and peace rather than one that would relieve the conditions of the laboring classes. For economic growth to occur, individual liberties had to be protected and coordinated, and man's propensities to truck and barter had to be given as much freedom as possible. This was best accomplished, he argued, through a form of government in which the judicial and executive branches were separated. This would in turn promote progress in commerce and industry while preserving personal liberty, security, and rule by law. It would also, however, reinforce the existing social hierarchy, with its impoverished, uneducated classes at the bottom and its educated wealthy at the top.

CIVILIZATION, INDUSTRY, AND PROGRESS

French and Scottish political economists coined the word *civilization* in the 1760s and 1770s to refute Jean Jacques Rousseau's charge that people were morally corrupted by life in civilized society and that neither greater learning nor the desire to be better than other people had improved the human condition. The political economists believed that "contemporary commercial society was the highest condition to which man could aspire and that such a society was a possible outcome—possible for all peoples everywhere—of a determinate, intelligible, and, to some degree, controllable, historical process."[22]

In this usage of *civilization,* polite or civil society was seen as distinguished from, although still dependent on the state. The earliest usage (in 1766) claimed that, "When a savage people has become civilized, we must not put an end to the act of *civilization* by giving it rigid and irrevocable laws; we must make it look upon the legislation given to it as a form of *continuous civilization.*" A year later, Abbé Baudeau wrote, "Land ownership ... constitutes a very important step toward the most perfect form of civilization." In 1770, Guillaume Raynal wrote, "The people who have polished [civilized] all others were merchants." In 1773, the Baron d'Holbach insisted that:

A nation becomes civilized through experiment.... Complete *civilization* of peoples and the leaders who govern them and the desired reform of governments, morals and abuses can only be the work of centuries, and the result of the constant efforts of the human spirit and the repeated experiments of society.[23]

In other words, civilization was created by men; it involved the development of their social condition as well as the refinement of their intellectual capacities.

Both the idea and the word rapidly became integral parts of the working vocabulary of the French and Scottish intelligentsia; in 1792 the newborn daughter of a French deputy was optimistically named "Civilisation." By the early 1800s, civilization was being viewed as both a *process* and an *achieved condition* characterized by social order, refined manners and behavior, and the accumulation of knowledge. It reflected the development of the human condition and intellect. By the 1820s, however, French commentators wondered whether there was such a thing as progress toward a universal civilization, or whether civilization was the product of particular peoples or nations at different times and places. Framing the question in this way quickly allowed them to make comparisons between past and present civilizations, and discussions dealing with the civilizations of ancient Greece, modern France, or Renaissance Europe soon appeared.[24] Both the word and the idea were pluralized.

Social and economic changes resulting from the growing importance of manufacturing were apparent in the Western European nations by 1830. Factories producing goods for domestic and foreign markets dotted the landscape from southern Scotland and the English Midlands to the Ruhr Valley. Rapid population growth had stimulated demand for the cloth and other goods available in the markets. Roads were extended, increasing in England, for instance, from 21,000 miles in 1800 to 170,000 miles in 1850. People were moving about on an unprecedented scale: 4 million Europeans immigrated to the Americas between 1816 and 1850, and an even larger number moved from one European country to another.[25]

The French intellectual and utopian socialist Henri Saint-Simon used the term *industrial society* to describe the new social order. From his viewpoint, the industrial system, unlike earlier forms of production,

Book plate showing Minerva, the Roman goddess of wisdom
and the arts, handing a book to a kneeling Indian, who offers
his tomahawk in exchange. The Latin motto, Emollit Mores
(Ovid) means "It makes one's behavior gentler." [Museum of
Fine Arts, Boston, M. And M. Karolik Collection.]

was built around the institutions of civil society, not the centralized political structures of the state. Civil society and the state were therefore separate, and the function of politics was to establish and maintain an equilibrium between economic and political institutions. Since industrial society was hierarchically organized, it was argued that social regulation should emanate from a moral center—an elite composed of scientists and industrialists. These social engineers would oversee planning, organization, and production.[26]

Some of Saint-Simon's ideas were elaborated upon by his former secretary Auguste Comte, who became a founder of nineteenth-century positivism and modern sociology. Comte was appalled by the actions of the French revolutionaries, who had attacked the traditional values of authority, morality, religion, and the family. His goal was to regenerate European civilization. However, he realized that it was impossible to return to the old order because of the social and economic changes that had occurred and the new social relations that were already in place. The impetus for regeneration had to come from the government, whose intellectuals (no longer the servants of the king, but now the emerging middle classes) were the ones best situated to promote morality, command obedience, and maintain social order.[27]

In Comte's view, the state intellectuals, by virtue of their actions and policies, would also promote the development of civilization, which was based on progress. Western European civilization stood at the top of a hierarchy of societies that stretched back in time to "a condition that was barely superior to that of a society of great apes."[28] For progress to occur, there must be social order, and when progress occurred, it further consolidated the society that had allowed it to unfold. The lower classes of Western Europe should therefore accept the fact that their social subordination was ordained by nature and acknowledge the superiority of their rulers.

SOCIAL EVOLUTION AND CIVILIZATION

Industrialization entered a new phase during the 1850s and 1860s in both Europe and the United States. It was characterized by the large-scale production of steel, which went into making rails, locomotives, and machines that were then used to produce other commodities. The concentration and centralization of capital underwrote the high cost of this form of production. In the United States, expenditures by the federal government during and after the Civil War contributed to the accumulated capital that made massive industrial development possible. The mid-nineteenth century was also a period of imperial expansion. Mexico, for instance, lost nearly half of its national territory to the United States as a result of a war that ended in 1848. Under the banner of Manifest Destiny, the westward expansion was portrayed as the realization of a divine mission by a racially superior, chosen people—white, Anglo-Saxon Christians—who had been chosen to conquer nature and bring civilization to the subordinated Indian tribes on the frontier and in the Indian territories.[29]

Many Western European and U.S. intellectuals believed that the superiority of civilization was the result of the natural process of social evolution. That is, the increasingly complex industrial societies of the nineteenth century had developed slowly, continuously, and differentially from the simpler societies of earlier times.[30] Social evolutionists, such as Herbert Spencer in England or Lewis Henry Morgan in the United States, argued that both the human and the natural worlds were governed by the same immutable laws of evolution. They defined progress as directional change—a slow, steady process that was unfolding on a global scale. However, they believed that progress was uneven in a double sense. Different societies and races were advancing at different speeds, and the pace at which a particular society developed varied during different stages of its evolution. They distinguished civilized societies from those that lacked state institutions and class structures, and claimed that the former were superior or more advanced than the latter. They used this claim to buttress a second claim: that there were social, cultural, and racial hierarchies.

This idea gained many adherents in the industrializing countries of Western Europe and the United States during the late nineteenth century. The idea was grounded in a belief that such hierarchies were the natural result of evolution—and, hence, of progress. They also believed that northern Europe and the United States were the most advanced nations: a Yale alumnus even argued that the particular conditions that promoted the development of the highest levels of civilization existed *only* in the environs of his *alma mater*.

Lewis Henry Morgan, who was mainly concerned with the development of human society, saw the evolutionary succession from savagery through barbarism to civilization as a generalization about human history. Not only did human society develop in this manner, but it could not have developed otherwise. Progress—the movement from one stage to the next—was the result of technological innovations that transformed the modes of subsistence and the social institutions that were inextricably linked to them. But while Morgan believed that progress was ultimately inevitable and beneficial, he also thought that the rise of civilization had destroyed something valuable: the values of those past and present-day peoples who knew neither private property nor the profit motive.[31]

Herbert Spencer and his followers drew no such clear distinction between human society, nature, and the cosmos, all of which, they believed, were subject to the same immutable laws. As a result, they saw the evolution of human society—the rise of civilization—as merely one aspect of a general tendency toward progress in the cosmos. Like Morgan, they interpreted progress as directional change: a slow, continuous movement from the simple to the complex, marked by steadily increasing differentiation as homogeneity was transformed into heterogeneity. In the human realm, progress was marked by an increasing division of labor, mutual dependence, and the rise of individualism. They believed this process was shaped by broadly defined ecological and social components of the environment that determined human physical and mental characteristics by permitting or constraining their use. They also believed that the industrialization of the Western imperialist countries marked the culmination or perfection of human happiness![32]

Spencer drew a sharp distinction between primitive and civilized man. In his view, the behavior, emotions, and intellect of primitive man were different from those of civilized man. They more closely reflected the natural environment. Primitives lacked curiosity, imagination, and the ability to think abstractly; they tended to be impulsive, antisocial, and deeply rooted in tradition. The reason was that they had simpler nervous systems, and this in turn was a result of their savage way of life. Civilized man, in contrast, was everything primitive man was not: curious, imaginative, and capable of abstract thought; he was social and receptive to change. In his view, the civilized child recapitulated all of the physical, emotional, and intellectual traits of primitive man during maturation.

SOCIAL DARWINISM AND CIVILIZATION

Spencer's views were very influential in both the United States and Europe. Here was a seemingly scientific validation for beliefs that considered the differences between individuals, societies, races, nations, and even corporations to be rooted in nature. This ideology, known as social Darwinism, interpreted the world in terms of the "survival of the fittest."[33] It was very influential between the 1880s and World War I, and was revived in the 1970s as sociobiology. While social Darwinism is not the same as Charles Darwin's theory of biological evolution, both build on the views of Thomas Malthus.

Social Darwinists believed that all things from organisms and human societies progressed naturally, from lower to higher or more advanced forms. They constructed various kinds of hierarchies to portray or represent the developmental relations of living organisms or human societies. In the circular logic of their view, the "fittest" forms were found at the top of those hierarchies, which was a sign that they were either more perfect or had progressed further up the evolutionary ladder. For example, Charles Darwin himself remarked that "a nation which produced during a lengthened period the greatest number of highly intellectual, energetic, brave, patriotic, and benevolent men, would generally prevail over less favored [i.e., less civilized] nations."[34] A U.S. Ambassador to England in the early 1840s declared that "the Anglo-Saxon race, from which we Americans trace our descent, is surpassed by none other that ever existed."[35] And John D. Rockefeller, Sr., a social Darwinist to the core, claimed that "the growth of a large business is merely the survival of the fittest ... merely the working out of a law of nature and a law of God."[36] Thus, the social Darwinists arranged nations, races, and even corporations in hierarchies.

Social Darwinists, echoing both Herbert Spencer and Charles Darwin, believed that civilizations were created by elites whose members prospered by knowing how to dominate subordinated classes and communities. In the United States, they were also closely attuned to the views of politicians and the businessmen who built museums, sponsored world's fairs, and used the stereotype of an uncivilized, homogenized American Indian society "as a baseline for measuring the extent of the material progress" they were creating.[37]

The ideology of social Darwinism was used to provide scientific legitimation for the existing class structure and social hierarchy. In the United States, it was used to justify claims of Anglo-American superiority and anti-immigrant sentiments in the North and racist policies in the South. It justified calls for imperialist wars, first against Native Americans in the Indian Territories and then in order to acquire territories in the Caribbean and the Pacific. After World War I, it buttressed congressional legislation that restricted immigration.

ECONOMIC GROWTH, NEO-EVOLUTION, AND CIVILIZATION

The use of evolution and progress as metaphors to describe human society waned after World War I. The brutality and human suffering the war had brought made it difficult to talk of human progress. Yet, after World War II the metaphors were revived, especially in the United States, which was one of the few industrial economies that was not damaged or destroyed by either war. After 1945, the United States, using arguments that echoed those of social Darwinists half a century earlier, began to project itself as the center and driving force of Western civilization.

In March 1947, President Harry Truman told the U.S. Congress that the Soviet Union was a threat to U.S. security, and that the United States would "support free peoples who resisted attempted subjugation by armed minorities and outside pressures."[38] A month later, financier and statesman Bernard Baruch described the hostile relationship between the United States and the Soviet Union as a "cold war"—a term seized on by the media. At the same time, the abridged version of Arnold Toynbee's *Study of History* (1947) made the bestseller list, where it stayed for months. Toynbee became a popular speaker on the lecture circuit, elaborating his views on the threat of "barbarism" and the crises that had led to the rise and fall of civilizations. Many in his audiences assumed he was talking about the cold war and came away from the lectures believing that this conflict threatened the existence of civilization itself.

Many officials in the U.S. government believed their mission was not only to preserve civilization but to spread it to the far corners of

the globe. This required that all Americans have a profound apprecia-
tion of the view that their society was not only exceptional but also
that its members were "chosen people," who had been selected by
God to carry out His civilizing mission. By virtue of their history, U.S.
citizens had successfully disassociated themselves from European
civilization, which stood in ruins after the war; as a result, America
now stood on the brink of re-instituting civilization on a new and
higher level.[39] Many U.S. academics and state officials were convinced
by the rhetoric of the cold war. They believed that American and
Western civilization was progressive while the USSR was an uncivilized
oriental despotism.[40] All the societies outside the political orbit of the
United States and its allies were considered backward, resembling
earlier stages in the social evolution of the West; they were frozen in
time as a result of their resistance to capitalist values or their inability
to purchase commodities. In turn, industrial capitalism was seen as
the highest development of civilization in both the material and moral
sense; progress was measured in terms of economic growth, which
relied on rebuilding and expanding the productive forces. By this logic,
the U.S. government would have to provide foreign aid to rebuild the
industrial economies of Japan and Western Europe, in order to ensure
the continued progress of Western civilization.

This project was buttressed by neo-evolutionary theories that saw
social change as moving only in one direction, and societies as becom-
ing increasingly differentiated. In contrast to nineteenth-century evo-
lutionism, which often focused on changes that affected humanity as
a whole, the neo-evolutionists were concerned with the development
of each separate society or civilization and with the causal mechanisms
underlying this. They developed elaborate historical theories about the
rise of civilization. For example, the anthropologist Julian Steward
described the political-economic mechanisms that linked ancient and
modern civilizations:

The rise and decline of the kingdoms in the ancient centers of civilization in Egypt, Mesopotamia, India, China, Meso-America, and the Andes is often described as the rise and fall of civilization. It is true that the particular kinds of societies found in these centers did not survive, but most of the basic cultural achievements, the essential features of civilization, were passed on to other nations. In each of these centers both culture and society changed rather considerably during the early periods, and everywhere the developmental processes were about the same. At first there were small communities of incipient farmers. Later the communities cooperated in the construction of irrigation works and the populations became larger and more settled. Villages amalgamated into states under theocratic rulers.... Finally culture ceased to develop, and the states of each area entered into competition with one another....

[A]n era of cyclical conquest followed. The conquests conformed to a fairly stable pattern.... Each state began to compete with others for tribute and advantages. One or another state succeeded in dominating the others, that is, in building an empire, but such empires ran their course and collapsed after some ... years only to be succeeded by another empire not very different from the first.

For the historian this era of cyclical conquests is filled with great men, wars and battle strategy, shifting power centers, and other social events. For the culture historian the changes are much less significant than those of the previous eras when the basic civilizations developed or, in the Near East, those of the subsequent Iron Age when the cultural patterns changed again and the centers of civilization shifted to new areas....

The industrial revolution brought profound cultural change to Western Europe and caused competition for colonies and for areas of exploitation. Japan entered the competition as soon as she acquired the general pattern. The realignments of power caused by Germany's losses in the first world war and by Italy's and Japan's in the second are of a social order. What new cultural patterns will result from these remains to be seen.

The general assumption today seems to be that we are in danger of basic cultural changes caused by the spread of communism. Russia acquired drastically new cultural patterns as a result of her revolution.

Whether communism has the same meaning in other nations has still to be determined.[41]

The political liabilities of such neo-evolutionary economic-growth theories became apparent in the mid-1950s. After the economies of Japan and Western Europe were rebuilt, the focus of U.S. foreign aid shifted to Africa, Asia, and the Middle East. In this context, questions of decolonization and economic development rather than reconstruction came to the fore. Both U.S. policies and the understanding of progress shifted when the USSR emerged as a second source of foreign aid, and the nations participating in the Bandung Conference advocated "nonalignment" with both the capitalist West and the communist USSR. In this milieu, merely developing the productive forces was no guarantee that the undeveloped and nonaligned nations could pursue capitalist development. Something else was needed.

MODERNIZATION, CONVERGENCE, AND CIVILIZATION

Spreading capitalist civilization to the third world was called "modernization." The word implied not only capitalist industrial development but also the transformation and replacement of traditional norms and practices in those societies. Now there would be production for profit, the concentration of the labor force in urban areas, the affirmation of reason and science and their application to production, bureaucratization, and a reliance on individual initiative. There would also be an increasingly unequal distribution of wealth among the various classes. To ensure that such modernization would actually happen, intellectuals like Walter Rostow or Clifford Geertz identified those classes in third world countries whose members would promote modernization by virtue of preferences and investment patterns. These were the groups that received U.S. aid and other forms of support.[42]

From this perspective, modernization was an inherently expansionary or globalizing process that would eventually incorporate larger and larger geographical areas. While modernity appeared first in the economic and political spheres, it quickly reached deep into the core of traditional societies affecting even the most intimate aspects of everyday life, such as religious beliefs, tastes, and leisure activities. Modernization was, by definition, an effort to reproduce capitalist social relations and culture in third world countries, but since it emanated from the industrial capitalist countries of the West, it was a homogenizing process aimed at making third world countries more like Western capitalist civilizations. By the late 1960s, Rostow, Samuel Huntington (discussed in Chapter 1) and others coined the term *convergence* to refer to the homogenizing—but not equalizing—effects of modernization.[43]

Modernization theory began to be criticized in the 1970s, first, not surprisingly, in the third world itself. The prediction that underdeveloped countries would come to resemble developed Western societies was not coming to pass, and more and more third world countries saw themselves instead being incorporated into a globalizing capitalist economy in a dependent role. Furthermore, since there were multiple pathways to modernization, countries that started at different points had different experiences. Convergence theory, which looked at the economy, politics, and culture separately, meant that similar economic structures could coexist with different political and cultural regimes. Finally, the mechanisms for achieving modernization that were proposed by the advocates of convergence theory bordered on technological determinism and were not sustained by the actual course of events in those countries. As a result of these criticisms, modernization and convergence as ways of describing development were dropped briefly during the early 1980s.

Modernization and convergence theory were revived after the disintegration of the USSR and the Eastern bloc in the late 1980s, and the rhetoric of "evil empires threatening world civilization" became more restrained. State intellectuals in the United States like Huntington once again argued that modernization theory might provide a useful model for socialist societies to adopt capitalism and enter the West. The crucial difference between these countries and those of the third world was their starting point in the process: whereas many third world countries were heavily rooted in traditional social orders, a number of the socialist countries had already industrialized and rejected traditionalism, even though they still lacked the modernity, that modern outlook, which could only be forged in a milieu shaped by capitalist culture and values. In this context, neo-convergence theory meant that the industrialized countries would become like one another in the future, but that they would increasingly diverge from the non- and semi-industrialized third world nations. Neo-convergence theory also suggested that the real problems in the world today would not be those between East and West, but rather the ones that have been developing between the affluent industrialized countries of the North and the poor ones of the South.[44]

In this chapter, we explored the idea of civilization and the political-economic and social milieu in which the Western idea of civilization emerged. We saw that embedded in the idea of civilization was a theory of history that explained the so-called progressive changes from a primary or original (primitive) condition to a more advanced one by means of moral, intellectual, and social progress. The idea of civilization was forged in societies whose ruling classes were obsessed with hierarchy and wanted to ensure that inequalities were perpetuated.

For nearly five centuries, ruling-class intellectuals—from Jean Bodin to Newt Gingrich—have sought to explain to their peers how the existing power relations came to be and why they are legitimate. They have provided us with historical accounts of the development of stratified societies that are characterized by the rule of law, sophisticated arts and letters, and the demise of tradition. They have assured us that the manners and morality of its upper classes are superior to those of its own uneducated masses and of the members of the nonstratified communities that live in nature—that is, in the wilderness beyond its frontiers.

From the 1600s onward, the boosters of Western civilization have viewed their own societies as being more advanced than those of the ancient world, and have sought to identify and explain the motors that powered the development of capitalist society. Today's popular views of civilization, including those of Newt Gingrich, have continued to stress its positive features—material improvement, progress, and modernity—and the conditions that promote them. Negative features—such as the increasing spiritual alienation and the economic impoverishment of a growing number of people—have been portrayed as transient phenomena that can be eliminated either by removing them from sight or by building prisons to house those sectors of the population that are not benefiting from the development of a capitalist civilization based on the consumption of commodities.

However, not everyone has viewed the rise of civilization in positive terms. Many Western intellectuals were critics of civilization and the state. Seeing the negative features, the contradictions, they were increasingly skeptical about the benefits that civilization supposedly brought in its wake.

CIVILIZATION
AND ITS CRITICS

Civilization's champions have claimed that the institutions and practices of the ruling classes and the state are desirable and necessary in that they maintain order and underwrite the conquest of nature. The values and practices cultivated by elite institutions and the state, it has been argued, promote reason and the rationality required to overcome the limitations imposed by nature and traditional beliefs. From this viewpoint, civilization marks the highest stage of social development—the end of history, as it were; and the civilizing process makes the world a better place in which to live. But not everyone has been as enchanted with civilization as the boosters described in the last chapter.

Critics with diverse points of views realized immediately that the rise of civilization was a process fraught with contradictions, and by the mid-1500s they had already begun to level charges against the emerging social order. On the one hand, they condemned the way civilizations dealt with colonial subjects and, by extension, with subordinated classes in the metropolitan countries; they indicted the genocidal and ethnocidal practices of colonial policy. On the other hand, they surveyed the dilemmas that accompanied the rise of civilization: increasing inequality coupled with steadily increasing alienation, immiseration, and repression of desire. They explored the cultural differences separating civilized and noncivilized peoples to show the barbarism of civilization itself.

Critics often interwove the two strands, thereby blurring the differences between them. In the process, they constructed increasingly devastating critiques of the new social order. There have always been alternative understandings of the meaning of civilization. This multiplicity of views has a lot to do with the fact that they express the sentiments of people who see their world differently from those who occupy the top rungs of the various social hierarchies advanced and perpetuated by Western civilization.

A SIXTEENTH-CENTURY CRITIQUE OF SETTLER-COLONIES

When Columbus returned to Hispaniola in 1495, he learned that the natives had murdered the men he left behind. This occurred when the Spaniards attempted to exact tribute payments from the indigenous communities. As Columbus and his forces struggled to restore order on the island during the next nine months, they captured hundreds of rebels—men, women, and children—who were ultimately shipped to slave markets in the Canary Islands and Europe. By 1500, Columbus had sent more than 2,000 American Indians to the slave markets, because they had threatened or resisted his efforts to establish a colony.[1]

For the Spanish settlers, newly arrived from Europe and averse to working with their own hands, the slave trade, combined with the resistance of the natives, produced a labor shortage in the colony. They

*Spanish colonizers hanging Indians and setting fire to their houses.
[Engraving from Bartolomé de las Casas, Den Spieghel vande
Spaensche tyrannie ... (Amsterdam, 1609).]*

used temporary grants from the Crown, called *encomiendas,* to force
local Indians to work for them. The *encomenderos*—the settlers holding
these grants—were assigned a group of Indians from whom they could
exact tribute and labor. In return for the grant, they were obliged to
defend the colony, and to protect their native subjects and instruct
them in the Christian religion. The encomenderos quickly sought
to make the grants hereditary.[2]

The Spanish king tried unsuccessfully to prevent the encomienda
system from being introduced into Mexico and the other mainland
colonies in the 1520s and 1530s. He opposed the system, because it
created a feudal nobility with an independent power base and source
of income in the colonies. The encomenderos challenged royal author-

ity and siphoned off revenues badly needed by the Crown. The king launched a new attack on the encomienda system in the 1540s, this time from a position of greater power. The New Laws, enacted in 1542, were buttressed by the arguments of Bartolomé de Las Casas, a Dominican friar supported by the Crown, who criticized the brutality and excesses of the encomenderos during the 1520s and 1530s. The New Laws abolished Indian slavery and made native peoples free vassals of the Crown. They also prohibited colonial officials and religious orders from holding encomiendas, banned the creation of new encomiendas, and stipulated that existing encomiendas would revert to the Crown when their current holders died.[3]

The New Laws provoked an intense policy debate. The encomenderos' spokesman was Juan Ginés de Sepúlveda, the king's chaplain and official historian. He argued that the system was just and that the encomenderos should continue to teach civilized ways and Christianity to the natives. He claimed that the Indians were barbarians—pre-social men who were more like a colony of bees than a civil society. As a result, they lacked laws and private property, and abused what possessions they did have since they practiced cannibalism and human sacrifice, and used precious metals to make idols. In his view, the native societies, even the highly stratified Aztecs, were slaves by nature, and hence inferior to the civilized Spanish colonists.[4]

Las Casas and Francisco de Vitoria presented the Crown's view. They separated the rights of the colonists from the need to civilize the Indians, and started with a different view of the Indians. They viewed the native peoples as barbarians—not because they were natural slaves, as Sepúlveda argued, but rather because they were not Christian and lacked a written language. In their view, the Indians were men with all the rights and duties of rational human beings. When they adopted Christianity, they would become civilized. The policies proposed by Las Casas contained four major points. First, the colonists should not have special economic and political rights. Second, they should not have the right to interfere in the lives of the native peoples. Third, native polities should be re-established and placed under the control of the Crown. Fourth, the Church should have a special right to teach in the native communities and convert them to Christianity.[5]

The influence of the Spanish debate over colonial institutions and practices extended far beyond Spain itself. English intellectuals concerned with expanding England's influence have looked favorably on the harsh views and policies of the encomenderos. Recall from chapter 2 that Sir Thomas Smith, one of the founders of sixteenth-century English colonial policy, viewed the Irish as a "barbarous and uncivilized people" incapable of being civilized. He depicted them in the same way Sepúlveda portrayed Native Americans. That Smith was killed by his Irish servants probably reinforced the English gentry's view that the Irish were indeed dangerous, uncivil barbarians.[6] As England's diplomatic relations with Spain deteriorated toward the end of the sixteenth century, its propagandists translated Las Casas's criticisms of the encomenderos' brutality without mentioning that England had already implemented the same policies in Ireland.

In the 1570s, residents of the Low Countries (the Netherlands, Belgium, and Luxembourg) rebelled against the policies of Philip II, who was attempting to strengthen Spain's control over the region and its people. Anti-Spanish, anti-Catholic, and antifeudal sentiments fueled the revolt. The rebels, some of whom viewed themselves as colonial subjects akin to those in the Americas, made use of Las Casas's condemnation of Spanish imperialism. In 1578, they published a Flemish translation of Las Casas's *Brief Relation of the Destruction of the Indies*. A second Flemish edition, entitled *The Mirror of Spanish Tyranny*, appeared a year later, at the same time that a French language translation was published in Antwerp. The translations of Las Casas— along with popular songs, poems, and pamphlets—fueled both anti-Spanish and anti-Catholic sentiments in the Low Countries during the struggle for independence.[7]

During the 1570s, the Spanish governor in the Low Countries dismissed the nobility as "beggars." When he used the term, he was not referring to requests for alms. What he meant was that they were acting in a rude, uncivilized way. The Dutch nobility adopted this term of contempt and made it a name for themselves and their anti-Spanish and anti-Catholic followers. It became a rallying cry, a form of identification, in the street songs and guerrilla theater of the day.[8]

A SIXTEENTH-CENTURY CRITIQUE OF CIVILIZED SOCIETY

Europe was wracked by sporadic civil wars during the 1570s and 1580s. They typically pitted the nobility against the monarch, townspeople, and peasants. They were also the religious wars of the Counter-Reformation that pitted Catholic against Protestant. Spain intervened in the French civil war, because it wanted a weak monarchy and the Protestant Huguenots defeated; England, which opposed Spain's intervention, sided with the Huguenots. There was widespread devastation as foreigners and mercenary armies swept back and forth across the French countryside. In August 1573, more than ten thousand Protestant townspeople were massacred in Paris, Rouen, and other cities during a single week. These were the conditions that provoked Jean Bodin, the Huguenot counsel to the king (mentioned in the last chapter), to write *The Six Books of the Republic* (1577), which defended the absolute authority of the monarch.[9]

However, Bodin was not the only author to comment on civil society during the 1570s and 1580s. Catholic and Huguenot propagandists churned out several thousand pamphlets and books, mostly written in the French vernacular rather than Latin, to explain their views and plans. Michel de Montaigne's *Essays* (1588) was the most significant commentary from the period. His ancestors were international fish and wine merchants who had purchased a titled estate near Bordeaux early in the sixteenth century, and Montaigne, like his father, was a provincial official. The composition of the family was diverse: Montaigne himself was Catholic, his mother's family were Spanish Jews, and several of his siblings were Huguenots. Montaigne's tolerance of religious differences and his opposition to the excesses of the various factions led him to occupy a critical middle ground during the civil wars. His tolerance was buttressed by an insatiable curiosity about the customs of American Indians. He read published accounts and visited Tupinamba Indians from Brazil who had been brought to Rouen in the 1550s, where they were abandoned and left to fend for themselves in a kind of ethnographic garden on the edge of town.[10]

Montaigne criticized the civilized societies of Europe when he compared them, unfavorably, with travelers' descriptions of the American Indians that portrayed them as generous, honest, and not desirous of others' goods. In his view, these noble savages resembled the original human community. In the *Essays,* he used nudity as a metaphor for the original societies living in freedom, according to "nature's first laws," while clothing marked the counterfeit world of civilized societies where social relations were veiled and deceptive. When addressing the literate middle layers of French society, Montaigne proclaimed

> Had I been placed among those nations which are still said to live in the freedom of nature's first laws, I assure you that I should very gladly have portrayed myself here as entire and wholly naked.[11]

Montaigne viewed the destruction of the American Indian societies and the disintegration of his own as signs of the sickness of civilized society, which increasingly cloaked itself with lies that hid reality and distorted nature's laws. The falsehoods that clothed civilized society were marks of "the first stage in the corruption of morals [which] is the banishment of truth."[12]

Montaigne also contrasted the Tupinamba, the Brazilian Indian culture first described in the 1550s, with the ideal civilized society constructed by Plato in *The Republic:*

> This is a nation, I should say to Plato, in which there are no sort of traffic, no knowledge of letters, no science of numbers, no name for magistrate or for political authority, no system of servitude, no riches or poverty, no contracts, no successions, no partitions, no occupations but leisure ones, no care for any but common kinship, no clothes, no metal; no use of wine or wheat. The very words that signify lying, avarice, envy, belittling, parody, unheard of. How far from this perfection would he find the republic that he imagined.[13]

Montaigne also observed that barbarians were originally any people who were not Greek. His contemporaries used this conception to create an unambiguous dichotomy between their own civilized society and other nations they typically portrayed as wild, cruel, or brutal. He argued that reason instead of prejudice should be used to judge what constituted barbarity. He questioned whether the cannibalism of the Tupinamba, which involved the ritual eating of a man after he had died, was as barbaric and horrible as European practices. He proclaimed that

> I think there is more barbarity in eating a man alive than in eating him dead; and in tearing by tortures and the rack a body still full of feeling, in roasting a man bit by bit, in having him bitten and mangled by dogs and swine (as we have not only read but seen within fresh memory, not among ancient enemies, but among neighbors and fellow citizens, and what is worse, on the pretext of piety and religion), than in roasting and eating him after he is dead.[14]

Montaigne concluded his essay entitled "Of Cannibals" with comments made by the Tupinamba in Rouen. Two remarks stood out in his memory:

... they thought it very strange that so many grown men, bearded, strong, and armed, who were around the king ... should submit to obey a child [the king].... [T]hey had noticed that there were among us men full and gorged with all sorts of good things, and that their other halves were beggars at their doors, emaciated with hunger and poverty; and they thought it strange that these needy halves could endure such an injutice, and did not take the others by the throat, or set fire to their houses.[15]

Montaigne's comparison of Tupinamba culture with that of Europe challenged any automatic assumption about the superiority of civilized society.

A RADICAL CRITIQUE OF CIVIL SOCIETY IN SEVENTEENTH-CENTURY ENGLAND

Bad harvests, rising prices, and heavy taxes during the late 1640s compounded the effects of the English civil war. The war was more than an indecisive struggle between the king and that part of Parliament representing the interests of wealthy merchants and the dissatisfied landed gentry. It also gave rise to the views of new religious communities and wandering "masterless" men and women who had been uprooted from their homes. Oliver Cromwell, the leader of Parliament's New Model Army, viewed the latter, particularly those groups called the Levellers and the Diggers, as "persons differing little from the beasts."[16]

Gerrard Winstanley, who became a leading spokesman for the Levellers and Diggers, developed a devastating critique of civil society in the late 1640s. Winstanley and other Digger squatters at St. George's Hill began tilling communal lands on April 1, 1649 to recover the "common treasury" that had been lost through the privatization of land. In the days that followed, the Diggers were attacked physically and legally by the local population whose actions were manipulated by members of the gentry and the clergy. Winstanley insisted that

> every man had an equall freedom given of his Maker to till the earth, and to have dominion over the beasts of the field, the fowls of heaven, and fish in the Seas.[17]

Winstanley believed that this right was dissolved by the introduction of private property, and that it was withheld from common folk by virtue of social and political arrangements that had been set in place by the Norman Conquest. He told the landed gentry that

> the power of enclosing land and owning property was brought into the creation by your ancestors by the sword; which first did murder their fellow creatures, men, and after plunder or steal away their land, and left this land successively to you, their children. And therefore, though you did not kill or thieve, yet you hold that cursed thing in your hand by the power of the sword; and so you justify the wicked deeds of your fathers, and that sin of your fathers shall be visited upon the head of you and your children to the third and fourth generation, and longer too, till your bloody and thieving power be rooted out of the land.[18]

Winstanley proceeded to argue that private property has impoverished common people and driven them to crime:

> This particular propriety of mine and thine hath brought in all miserye upon people. For, first it hath occasioned people to steal from one another. Secondly, it hath made laws to hang those that did steal. It tempts people to do an evil action and then kills them for doing it.[19]

Private property, in his view, had different consequences for the rich, who believed that their right to dominate others was part of the natural order:

> The man of the flesh judges it a righteous thing that some men are clothed with the objects of the earth and so called rich men whether it be got by right or wrong should be magistrates to rule over the poor; and that the poor should be servants, nay rather slaves of the rich.[20]

In a hierarchically organized society, where land was privately owned and privilege was unevenly distributed, Winstanley asserted that law functioned to preserve the existing social relations:

> The Kingly power sets up a Law and Rule of Government to walk by; and here Justice is pretended but the full strength of the Law to uphold the conquering Sword and to preserve his son Propriety.... For though they say the Law doth punish yet indeed the Law is but the strength, life, and marrow of the Kingly power upholding the Conquest still, hedging some into the Earth, hedging out others; giving the Earth to some and denying the Earth to others which is contrary to the Law of Righteousnesse who made the Earth at first as free for one as for another.[21]

Winstanley argued that government did not rest on coercion alone; it also involved acquiescence to the existing social order. From his perspective, the clergy was largely responsible for depriving common people of education and for teaching them to accept their lot in life as a sign of God's will. He further remarked that the clergy continually repudiated the fundamental precepts of Christianity by their actions, and that they were rewarded by the nobility and the state; in his view, "there was a confederacie between the Clergy and the great red Dragon [the ruling class and the state]."[22] In spite of his criticisms of the clergy, Winstanley drew inspiration from the prophetic tradition of the Bible. He called Christ "the Head Digger," and identified the poor with the Jews of the Exodus narrative—that is, persecuted, landless strangers in a foreign land.[23]

Winstanley believed that the solution to England's social problems required the abolition of private ownership of the means of production and its products. These, he argued, should be held in common and freely distributed. However, his arguments were quickly muted with the Restoration, which was essentially a compromise that allowed the gentry and middle classes to exploit economic opportunities and prevented the royal family and the Church from blocking progress.

ROUSSEAU AND THE ROMANTIC CRITIQUE
OF CIVILIZATION

The word *civilization* was coined in the 1760s by Enlightenment boosters who claimed "that contemporary commercial society was the highest condition to which man could aspire and that such a society was a possible outcome—possible for all peoples everywhere—of a determinate, intelligible, and, to some degree, controllable, historical process."[24] The Enlightenment was a time when elites from Mexico City to Moscow sought to sever the customary, mutually recognized obligations they had toward members of the lower classes and to install in their place a civil society—one in which social relations would be based on the principles of market exchange. While the intellectuals employed by these elites agreed in their criticisms of the old social order, they disagreed on how and what kinds of change should be brought about. One group, whose members promoted the liberalism of John Locke, advocated parliamentary forms of government that would secure and protect the rights of estates and individuals. The members of the second group promoted the opinions of Francis Bacon and Voltaire who advocated an enlightened despotism—a planned society ruled by experts.[25]

The social critic Jean Jacques Rousseau disagreed with both groups and staked out a third position that echoed the views of Montaigne and Winstanley and effectively framed modern discussions of civilization. In his *A Discourse on the Moral Effects of the Arts and Sciences* (1750), Rousseau charged that people were morally corrupted by life in civilized society and that neither progress in learning nor the desire to be better than others have improved the human condition:

> The politicians of the ancient world were always talking of morality and virtue; ours speak of nothing but commerce and money.[26]

> So long as government and law provide for the security and well-being of men in their common life, the arts, literature, and the sciences, less

despotic though perhaps more powerful, fling garlands of flowers over the chains which weigh them down. They stifle in men's breasts that sense of original liberty ... [and] make of them what is called a civilized people.

Necessity raises up thrones; the arts and sciences have made them strong. Powers of the earth, cherish all talents and protect those who cultivate them. Civilized people cultivate such pursuits: to them, happy slaves, you owe that delicacy and exquisiteness of taste, which is so much your boast, that sweetness of disposition and urbanity of manners which makes intercourse so easy and agreeable among you—in a word, the appearance of all the virtues, without being in possession of one of them....[27]

The classic bourgeois family, eighteenth century France.
[Culver Pictures, Inc.]

In the next few years, Rousseau focused on the issue of inequality and its consequences, suggesting that

> The first source of evil is inequality. From inequality came wealth, for the words rich and poor are relative, and whenever men were equal there were no rich and poor. From wealth was born luxury and idleness. From luxury, the fine arts were born. From idleness, the sciences....[28]

In the *Discourse on the Origin of Inequality* written in 1755, he noted that the development of civilization

> gave new powers to the rich; which irretrievably destroyed natural liberty, eternally fixed the law of property and inequality, converted clever usurpation into unalterable right, and, for the advantage of a few ambitious individuals, subjected all mankind to perpetual labour, slavery, and wretchedness.[29]

He noted that the civilizing process had different effects on the members of the lower classes and the ruling elites and argued that civilization had different implications for them.

> The former breathes only peace and liberty; he desires only to live and be free from labour.... Civilized man, on the other hand, is always moving, sweating, toiling and racking his brains to find still more laborious occupations.... He pays court to men in power, whom he hates, and to the wealthy, whom he despises; he stops at nothing to have the honour of serving them; he is not ashamed to value himself on his own meanness and their protection; and, proud of his slavery, he speaks with disdain of those, who have not the honour of sharing it.... [T]he source of all these differences is ... [that the civilized] man only knows how to live in the opinion of others....[30]

Rousseau's critique of the emerging social order was, and still is, a devastating judgement of civilization. He challenged powerful claims about the benefits that allegedly accrued from the conquest of nature and the development of an increasingly industrial civilization—at the very moment that industrial capitalism, that possessive market society, was experiencing a phase of explosive growth in northwestern Europe. He was skeptical of assertions that civilization was beneficial—that is, that it improved the condition of humanity. Instead, he drew attention to the values that were lost to the world with the rise of civilization, which brought inequality and alienation in their wake. The memory of those values—and of that lost world where inequalities and alienation were not so marked or did not exist—was kept alive by those men and women who were vanquished in the civilizing process. Meanwhile, those values were followed and protected by the barbarians who had yet to experience the devastating effects of civilization. Hence Rousseau's discourses should not be misunderstood as an expression of some sentimental desire to return to an idyllic past.

A LATE EIGHTEENTH-CENTURY NATIONALIST CRITIQUE OF CIVILIZATION

Johann Herder, a school teacher whose writings laid the foundations for nationalism, was highly critical of the predominant Enlightenment view of civilization. This view, he argued, conflated "culture with civilization and intellectual sophistication, opposing it to the original simplicity of nature."[31] *Culture,* which had originally meant the art of cultivation or growing something in the soil, became a metaphor referring to the process of cultivating the human mind in the 1600s. By 1800, *culture* referred to both the process and the condition that occurred when the manners of men and women were polished or refined by education (the civilizing process). Thus, being cultured had definite class connotations, where only persons of privilege with financial means and leisure were able to pursue aesthetic, moral, and intellectual activities in their quest for perfection.[32]

Herder's criticisms of civilization arose from his experiences in the petty, German-speaking states of central Europe during the 1770s and

1780s, and were part of a wider critique of the social and political conditions that prevailed in the German-speaking areas. His chief targets were feudalism, the hereditary nobility, censorship, and the state. In 1789, Herder was an outspoken supporter of the French Revolution, the Declaration of the Rights of Man, the abolition of feudalism, and the dismantling of the absolutist monarchy. In September of that year, Herder shared his views on the Revolution with members of the German nobility; he called the court "a scabhead and the courtiers the louses that crawled over it."[33]

Herder was also vexed by Enlightenment intellectuals who legitimated the subordination and exploitation of non-European peoples with claims about the superiority of European civilization. He was especially irked by social commentators, like John Millar, whose historical writings portrayed European civilization of the Enlightenment as the highest stage of social development. He wrote that they supported oppression and served to maintain the status quo:

> The universal dress of philosophy and philanthropy can conceal repression, violations of the true personal, human, local, civil, and national freedom, much as Cesare Borgia would have liked it.[34]

In contrast to the predominant Enlightenment opinion, Herder distinguished civilization from culture. Civilization was seen as something mechanical associated with the state, and the civilizing process erased people's knowledge and experiences of everyday life. For instance, the state attempted to impose French, the language of the court, onto other areas of daily life. Herder believed that language was fundamental to social interaction and education; it was the means by which individuals became aware of their inner selves and conscious of those who spoke other languages. Thus, there was a close connection between a community's language, its shared patterns of thought, and everyday life—that is, its culture. In other words, the culture of a people (*Volk*) was a contingent, complex whole; language was the most basic element of this configuration and the most distinctive feature of a people's cultural heritage. Culture, unlike civilization, was marked by spontaneity, earthiness, and natural simplicity.

For Herder, culture was both a national unit and a relatively unstratified community. It consisted of those who were governed: the burghers—the farmers, craftsmen, and traders, who were least affected by civilization—and the intellectuals. It included neither the aristocrats who ruled nor an ill-defined but clearly demarcated rabble at the other end of the social spectrum. While Herder was opposed to hereditary class hierarchy, he argued that popular leaders, "men of the people," originated in the middle classes and that "intellectual and cultural activity has its source in the middle class; in order to re-vitalize the whole of the people it will need to become diffused in both the upward and downward direction."[35] These popular leaders should strive to make the existing political order more humane, which would pave the way for the dissolution of the state as an administrative machine and for the emergence of an organic "ordering of social life, in which active co-operation would render all forms of sub-ordination obsolete and superfluous."[36]

His critique of the state was that it failed to help its citizens develop their physical, emotional, intellectual, aesthetic, moral, and political propensities. By neglecting the cultivation of its subjects, the state deprived itself of valuable resources and, ultimately, endangered its own existence.

> To fail to make use of man's divine and noble gifts, to allow these to rust and thus to give rise to bitterness and frustration, is not only an act of treason against humanity, but also the greatest harm which a State can inflict upon itself; for what is lost with such "dead" and "buried" assets is not merely the capital including the interest. Since in actual fact these assets are life forces, they invariably defy burial and hence tend to create a great deal of confusion and disturbance in the body politic. An unemployed human being cannot rest, simply because he is alive, and in his frustration

he is likely to use his gifts for destructive ends. Social and political chaos is the inevitable outcome of this human tragedy.[37]

He was keenly aware of the linkages between the availability of education, economic opportunities, and the potential for political unrest. Herder believed the state should take responsibility for the *humanization* of its subjects. That is, it should provide education and ensure a certain level of welfare. In his terms, "A country needs not only letters but also bread."[38] The process of humanization involved the development of the self, not only as an individual, but more importantly as the member of a community. To achieve their fullest potential, individuals must actively cooperate with one another and with the wider community. This humanization would be led by those "men of the people," rather than by the state and its ruling class; their function was "to shorten the path... [but not to] attempt to carry us lest we should thereby become paralyzed."[39]

Herder's goal was a world with numerous nations, each a *Volk* with its own distinctive culture and experiences. His model was the tribal society of the ancient Jews, particularly descriptions rooted in the prophetic tradition as opposed to those set down by priests or royal scribes.[40] These nations would be integrated by shared cooperative activity based on the moral consciousness of their members rather than by the direction and laws of the state. Unlike civilizations, these steps would promote humanization within the nation and between different nations.

Intellectuals influenced by Herder (and Rousseau) further explored the linkages between civilization and culture by virtue of the contrasts they drew. In 1830, Samuel Taylor Coleridge, the English Romantic poet and social critic who once described the plight of overcivilized, uncultivated young men, wrote:

A nation can never be too cultivated, but may easily become an over-civilized race. The permanency of the nation ... and its progressiveness and personal freedom ... depend on a continuing and progressive civilization. But civilization is itself but a mixed good, if not far more a corrupting influence, the hectic of disease, not the bloom of health, and a nation so distinguished more fitly to be called a varnished than a polished people, where this civilization is not grounded in cultivation, in the harmonious development of those qualities and faculties that characterize our humanity.[41]

Since the 1830s, German social critics have more faithfully maintained the distinction between culture and civilization than their French, English, and American contemporaries.

MARX, ENGELS, AND THE RADICAL CRITIQUE OF CIVILIZATION

Karl Marx and Frederick Engels viewed civilization as a particular form of society, one characterized by class divisions and a state apparatus that maintained the existing relations of inequality. They launched their critique of capitalist civilization in the 1840s. In the *Manifesto of the Communist Party* (1848), they described the impact of capitalist development on civilization at home and abroad.

All old-established national industries have been destroyed or are daily being destroyed. They are dislodged by new industries, whose introduction becomes a life and death question for all *civilised* nations, by industries that no longer work up indigenous raw material, but raw material drawn from the remotest zones; industries whose products are consumed, not only at home, but in every quarter of the globe. In place of the old wants, satisfied by the productions of the country, we find new wants, requiring for their satisfaction the products of distant lands and climes. In place of the old local and national seclusion and self-sufficiency, we have intercourse in every direction, universal inter-dependence of nations. And as in material, so also in intellectual production. The intellectual creations of individual nations become common property. National one-sidedness and narrow-mindedness become more and more impossible, and from the numerous national and local literatures, there arises a world literature.

The bourgeoisie, by the rapid improvement of all instruments of production, by the immensely facilitated means of communication, draws all, even the most barbarian, nations into civilisation. The cheap prices of its commodities are the heavy artillery with which it batters down all Chinese walls, with which it forces the barbarians' intensely obstinate hatred of foreigners to capitulate. It compels all nations, on pain of extinction, to adopt the bourgeois mode of production; it compels them to introduce what it calls civilisation into their midst, i.e., to become bourgeois themselves. In one word, it creates a world after its own image....

Modern bourgeois society with its relations of production, of exchange and of property, a society that has conjured up such gigantic means of production and of exchange, is like the sorcerer, who is no longer able to control the powers of the nether world whom he has called up by his spells. For many a decade past the history of industry and commerce is but the history of the revolt of modern productive forces against modern conditions of production, against the property relations that are the conditions for the existence of the bourgeoisie and of its rule. It is enough to mention the commercial crises that by their periodical return put on its trial, each time more threateningly, the existence of the entire bourgeois society. In these crises a great part not only of the existing products, but also of the previously created productive forces, are periodically destroyed. In these crises there breaks out an epidemic that, in all earlier epochs, would have seemed an absurdity—the epidemic of over-production. Society suddenly finds itself put back into a state of momentary barbarism; it appears as if a famine, a universal war of devastation cut off the supply of every means of subsistence; industry and commerce seem to be destroyed; and why? Because there is too much civilisation, too much means of subsistence, too much industry, too much commerce.[42]

Marx and Engels also pointed out in the *Manifesto* that capitalism was merely the latest form of civilization. In Western Europe, its appearance coincided with the dissolution of the tributary social relations that marked feudalism. They amplified their discussion of other forms of civilization in the 1880s. Marx scrutinized the ethnological writings of the day, and Engels produced *The Origin of the Family, Private Property, and the State* (1884).[43] In this period, Engels described the rise of civilization in the following manner:

> Civilization is ... the stage of development in society at which the division of labor, the exchange between individuals arising from it, and the commodity production which combines them both come to their full growth and revolutionizes the whole of previous society.[44]

> The power of the primitive community had to be broken. But it was broken by influences which from the very start appear as a degradation, a fall from the simple moral greatness of the old gentile [i.e., kin-organized] society. The lowest interests—base greed, brutal appetites, sordid avarice, selfish robbery of the common wealth—inaugurated the new, civilized, class society. It is by the vilest means—theft, violence, fraud, treason—that the old classless gentile society is undermined and overthrown.[45]

Engels explored the relation between the formation of social classes and the state. He astutely observed that societies existed without the state, and that the state appeared when societies became hierarchically organized.

> The state ... has not existed from all eternity. There have been societies which have managed without it, which had not notion of the state or state power. At a definite stage of economic development, which necessarily involved the cleavage of society into classes, the state became a necessity because of this cleavage....[46]

After observing that slavery, commerce, and exploitation attained their fullest development under civilization, Engels observed that:

> The stage of commodity production with which civilization begins is distinguished economically by the introduction of (1) metal money and with it money capital, interest and usury, (2) merchant as the class of intermediaries between the producers, (3) private ownership of land and

the mortgage system, (4) slave labor as the dominant form of production. The form of family corresponding to civilization and coming to definite supremacy with it is monogamy, the domination of the man over the woman and the single family as the economic unit of society. The central link in civilized society is the state, which in all typical periods is without exception the state of the ruling class and in all cases continues to be essentially a machine for holding down the oppressed, exploited class.[47]

Neither Marx nor Engels provided detailed blueprints for alternatives to capitalist civilization or how to achieve them. However, because of their studies of history and imperial expansion, they realized further social development would be contingent and would necessarily involve struggle. Throughout their careers, they frequently employed the idea of dialectical return, most characteristically in the form of *communism:* " ... the return of the absence of private property and classless division of labor characteristic of primitive societies, but associated with the productive capacities of capitalism."[48] In fact, both Marx and Engels turned their attention to primitive communal societies and precapitalist states in their last years, which coincided with a burst of imperial expansion from Europe into Africa and by the United States in Latin America, the Pacific, and its own Indian territories.

LIBERAL CRITIQUES OF CIVILIZATION

Liberal critics of civilization were already questioning the kind of society that was crystallizing in the mid-nineteenth century, when the social Darwinists proclaimed the inevitability of a West-centered civilization and progress. In the 1830s, John Stuart Mill, social critic and employee of the British East Indies Company, commented on the consequences of capitalist development for Western civilization and culture:

Take for instance the question of how far mankind has gained from civilization. One observer is forcibly struck by the multiplication of physical comforts; the advancement of and diffusion of knowledge; the decay of superstition; the facilities of mutual intercourse; the softening of manners; the decline of war and personal conflict; the progressive limitation of the tyranny of the strong over the weak; the great works accomplished throughout the globe by the co-operation of the multitudes.... Another fixes his attention, not upon the value of these advantages, but upon the high price which is paid for them; the relaxation of individual energy and courage; the loss of proud and self-relying independence; the slavery of so large a portion of mankind to artificial wants; the dull unexciting monotony of their lives, and the passionless insipidity, and absence of any marked individuality in their character; the contrast between the narrow mechanical understanding, produced by a life spent in executing by fixed rules a fixed task, and the varied powers of the man in the woods, whose subsistence and safety depend at each instant upon his capacity of extemporarily adapting the means to ends; the demoralizing effect of great inequalities in wealth and social rank; and the sufferings of the great mass of the people of civilized countries, whose wants are scarcely better provided than those of the savage, while they are bound by a thousand fetters in lieu of the freedom and excitement which are his compensations.[49]

By the beginning of the twentieth century, liberal critics had already built on Mill's insights into the contradictions of Western civilization. They increasingly believed that progress resulting from the production of wealth was merely an optimistic illusion. The deep economic recessions in the 1880s and 1890s suggested to them instead that the production of wealth occurred in short bursts that were inevitably followed by periods of stagnation. As a result of these cycles, "the continents are strewn with the ruins of dead nations and civilizations."[50] For some critics, particularly liberal theologians in the United States, the earlier civilizations failed because the new wealth they created was not evenly distributed. While some members of those societies became immensely wealthy, the vast majority languished in

slavery or poverty. The wealthy protected their immoral appropria-
tions by unjust laws, political centralization, and suppression of the
masses. The injustices of civilization were demoralizing.

For the liberal theologians, the only hope for regenerating the
modern social order would be to reestablish a moral presence. This
might be accomplished if the Church would inspire, but not attempt
to control, social movements that were simultaneously concerned with
reassessing values and with promoting conditions that would favor a
more equitable distribution of property and wealth. In this view, the
theoretical and political underpinnings for liberation theology of the
1970s and 1980s are found.[51]

Sigmund Freud, one of the founders of psychoanalysis, realized that
the ideals of civilization and human progress were badly damaged by
the brutality of World War I and the suffering it spawned. In *Civilization
and Its Discontents* (1930), he explored how the "later accretions of
civilization" were stripped away by the war to reveal the savage or
primal elements that were present even in the most civilized societies.[52] The mutual hostility of human beings threatened the very fabric
of civilization itself. Thus, since their instinctual passions overrode
reason, "civilization has to use its utmost in order to set limits to man's
aggressive instincts and to hold the manifestations of them in
check...."[53]

In Freud's view, civilization involved the use of science and technol-
ogy to harness nature as well as the adjustment of social relations to
maintain order. It was

> all those respects in which human life has raised itself above its animal
> status.... It includes on the one hand all the knowledge and capacity that
> men have acquired in order to control the forces of nature and extract its
> wealth for the satisfaction of human needs, and, on the other hand, all the
> regulations necessary in order to adjust the relations of men to one another
> and especially the distribution of available wealth.[54]

Civilization, which had significant class and cultural dimensions, was something "imposed on a resisting majority by a minority who understood how to obtain possession of the means to power and coercion."[55] Since the control of the masses by the minority was necessary, coercion was an indispensable tool for the more civilized classes, because the

> masses are lazy and unintelligent; they have no love for instinctual renunciation, and they are not to be convinced by argument of its inevitability; and the individuals composing them support one another in giving free reign to their indiscipline. It is only through the influence of individuals who can set an example and whom the masses recognize as their leaders, that they can be induced to perform the work and undergo the renunciations on which the existence of civilization depends.[56]

However, Freud believed that coercion was potentially dangerous, because it could provoke the hostility of the masses, especially

> If ... a culture has not got beyond the point at which the satisfaction of one portion of its participants depends upon the suppression of another, and perhaps larger portion—it is understandable that the suppressed people should develop an intense hostility toward a culture whose existence they make possible by their work, but in whose wealth they have too little a share.[57]

In Freud's view, the major problem confronting contemporary civilization remained in the realm of social relations: How to establish and maintain justice, equality before the law, for civilized peoples. He suggested that the problem might be remedied by

> a re-ordering of human relations ... which would remove the sources of dissatisfaction by renouncing coercion and the suppression of the instincts, so that undisturbed by internal discord, men might devote themselves to the acquisition of wealth and its enjoyment.[58]

This would mean that the pleasure brought by realization of human needs, such as order and cleanliness, could no longer be subordinated to the demands of civilization. It would also mean that those groups entering the civilized community would trade individual liberty for security and renounce certain forms of pleasure. The power of the individual would be replaced by a social contract that involved an entire community dedicated to the principle of

> justice—that is, the assurance that a law once made will not be broken in favour of an individual. This implies nothing as to the ethical value of such a law.... The final outcome should be a rule of law to which all—except those who are not capable of entering a community [i.e., the mad, women, and children]—have contributed by a sacrifice of their instincts, and which leaves no one—again with the same exception—at the mercy of brute force.[59]

Freud's pessimism about the effects of the class structure of civilization led him to believe that

> The final course of cultural development seems to tend towards making the law no longer an expression of the will of a small community—a caste or a stratum of the population or a racial group—which, in its turn, behaves like a violent individual towards other, and perhaps more numerous, collections of people.[60]

THE CULTURAL CRITIQUES OF CIVILIZATION

Unlike Freud's assessment which conflated culture and civilization, Friedrich Nieztsche's commentary on Western civilization in the 1880s was a cultural critique. His targets were simultaneously modern science, Christianity, and the dominant conception of classical Greek culture that underpinned Western civilization. These had become so intertwined over the centuries, in his view, that they fixed truth and homogenized it to serve the interests of the nation and the state. Western culture—which had once been a powerful, progressive force—had stagnated; consequently, it was no longer advantageous to cling to values rooted in European history. While pre-Socratic Greek culture had been authentic, the culture of modern capitalist West was not; it was instead a unity of pieces, flying in different directions, that were ultimately held together by manufactured, popular opinion.

Unfortunately, in Nietzsche's view, the modern culture brokers who manufactured consent for Western civilization were philistines—that is, they were barbarians who confused conformism with genuine culture and believed, because of their false consciousness, that they were cultured and refined like the educated elite of classical times. They continued to reproduce a set of values which proclaimed that the world and morality were both unchanging and unchangeable. However, the language and the concepts they used to understand themselves and others were so narrow that they provided no clarity for either comprehending or explaining the world around them. Nietzsche proposed to analyze their claims—their illusions and prejudices which served to fix social relations and promote nihilism.[61]

Nietzsche believed that the West needed new values that would protect the truly creative individual. These values could be found through a philosophical reworking of the culture of pre-Socratic Greece. While Nietzsche himself did not provide an alternative to the claims of the culture brokers, the views and methods he used to unravel their language and concepts have been adopted by contemporary social critics, like Michel Foucault. As a result, his concerns over relativism and the politics of morality have been basic to many of the postmodern critiques of contemporary Western culture.[62]

Arnold Toynbee, philosopher of history and popular lecturer, furnished a different cultural critique of Western civilization from that of Nietzsche in the years immediately after World War II. He based his views on a comparative study of more than twenty ancient and modern civilizations. Civilizations, in Toynbee's view, appeared and grew when the creative minority of a community successfully and repeatedly met the challenges of their environment. When this process ceased—and it did in every instance—the civilization broke down and began to disintegrate. As these civilizations fell apart, Toynbee postulated, their dominant minorities (rulers) sought to establish universal, all-powerful states, while the internal proletariats (the majority of the population) attempted to found universal churches: Christianity, Islam, etc. The external proletariats—that is, those marginalized by the collapse of the civilization and rise of the universal states—resisted and attacked the decaying civilization from the outside.

After the devastation left by World War II, Toynbee argued that the world was in crisis. In the wake of the Holocaust, he pointed to the continued aggression of Western civilization as the problem that the rest of the world was being driven to respond to. Hope for salvation was only to be found in a convergence of the great religions of the surviving civilizations—Christianity, Islam, Hinduism, and Buddhism—by constructing bridges between them. Otherwise, he feared, spiritual and creative progress would be hopeless; the world's people would be forced to rely on the drives and instincts described by Hobbes and Freud.[63]

SUMMARY

In this chapter, we examined various critiques of civilization and the milieu in which they emerged. Critics began to formulate unflattering assessments of Western civilization in the sixteenth century—that is, at the same time the idea of civilization itself was invented by the boosters and legitimizers of hierarchically organized societies and ruling class culture. From the 1540s onwards, the critics of civilization questioned whether the institutions, culture, and morality of the European states were superior to those of the non-Western (primitive) peoples they encountered in their American, African, or Asian colonies. Critics used ethnographic descriptions of these peoples as well as of their own peasantries to challenge the alleged superiority of the civilized classes and states. Many critics drew a distinction between civilization and culture.

Some (like Winstanley or Herder) who were critical of organized religion drew images from those sections of the Bible describing the activities of prophets and the communities they inspired. Others rooted their discussions of exploitation and oppression in terms of social and political-economic theory or culture. Romantic and nationalist critiques, stressing the role of creativity and spontaneity, appeared by the end of the eighteenth century. Liberal critiques, usually emphasizing the threat exploitation posed to the maintenance of social order, emerged along with industrial capitalism in the nineteenth century. Radical critiques, emphasizing exploitation and unequal social relations within the community, appeared at the same time. Cultural critiques of civilization, focused on modernity and the activities of civilization's boosters, were launched toward the end of the nineteenth century.

INVENTING BARBARIANS AND OTHER UNCIVILIZED PEOPLES

Civilization, as we have seen, always involves hierarchically organized social relations and cultures. A civilization is a class-stratified society that "civilization originates in conquest abroad and repression at home."[1] Its rise is intimately linked with the formation of social classes and a state apparatus. As part of the civilizing process, the politically dominant groups strive to distinguish themselves socially and culturally, both from classes that their members have subordinated at home and from communities beyond their frontiers. They portray their own members as *refined, polished,* and *cultured;* members of the subordinated classes and external communities are depicted in oppositional terms, as *uncivilized, barbaric, crude, rustic, wild,* or *savage.* The precise characterization is historically contingent, varying from one civilization to another.

The most important consequence of this labeling is that dominant groups tend to homogenize other classes and communities, stressing only a single dimension of their substance. In the process, the civilized impoverish their own understanding of these other groups and obscure their own affinity with them. Ultimately, this fuels their fear of these groups, from whom they seize goods and labor.

For the past 500 years, both boosters and critics of civilization have drawn their images of uncivilized peoples from the impressions and arguments of earlier authorities, including the Bible and classical writers such as Aristotle. These earlier sources discussed government, good and evil, peace and war, order and disorder; they wrote about nature, man, and society; and they crafted metaphors rich in meaning—like barbarians, gardens, ruins, or wildernesses—that still evoke powerful images even today. When intellectuals recovered these sources, acknowledged their authoritative status, and translated them into the vernacular languages of Western Europe, they ensured that the Scriptures and classical writers would continue to play prominent roles in intellectual, moral, social, and political debates of the day. Thus, long-dead authorities, writing about their own societies, provided the modern boosters and critics of civilization with a pool of ideas, images, and metaphors they could draw upon and recycle.

The early authorities did not have a monolithic viewpoint. One reason is that civilization is above all else a complex whole, composed of various groups, classes, and communities with different relations to power. Intellectuals voicing the sentiments and understandings of different constituencies usually have divergent understandings of the whole.

A second reason is that some early sources are, in fact, compilations of the views of different groups. The Scriptures, the most authoritative of all old sources, are perhaps the most widely cited compilation.[2] As a result,

The Bible could mean different things to different people at different times, in different circumstances. There are few ideas in whose support a Biblical text cannot be found. Much could be read into and between the lines.[3]

Yet a third reason is that in any generation, circumstances and practices link readers to these early texts in particular ways, shaping how readers understand them. Readers who interpret texts act as critics, viewing the texts through different lenses and moving the interpretive process in new or different directions. As a consequence, a text takes on multiple meanings that have to be assessed in light of current circumstances.[4]

In this chapter, we will examine how authorities have invented, refined, and recycled ideas about barbarians and other uncivilized peoples.

Class, gender, ethnicity, and race are historically and socially constructed distinctions, rather than categories that occur naturally. However, it is useful to remember that both the boosters and critics of civilization have traditionally either opposed civilization to nature or claimed that it developed out of nature, usually through a series of stages or under certain circumstances. As a result, the idea of nature, which plays an important role in both scenarios, "contains ... an extraordinary amount of human history."[5] It is a complicated idea that has long had two simultaneous usages: (1) the inherent, essential character or qualities of something; and (2) "the multiplicity of things, and of living processes ... organized around a single essence or principle: a nature."[6] Since discussions about nature and humanity's relation to it are ultimately about knowledge and control, they cannot be separated from the interests of the individuals and groups that made them.

BEASTS, BARBARIANS, AND WOMEN
IN CLASSICAL GREECE

The *Iliad* and *Odyssey,* the heroic poems composed by Homer in the Aegean islands before 700 b.c., are our earliest sources of information about Greek social thought. Recited by traveling bards to gatherings, these poems provide glimpses of the social conditions in the Aegean area before the first *poleis,* or city-states, appeared on the western frontier of the Neo-Assyrian empire. At the time, the Neo-Assyrians controlled much of the Near East, the independent Phoenician cities in what is now Lebanon and Israel, and a politically weakened Egypt.

The poems describe communities that lacked political centralization; whatever power the chieftains, warlords, or elders possessed rested to a considerable extent on their ability to persuade their kin and neighbors that the courses of action they proposed were appropriate.[7] Human beings were distinguished from one another by status and gender, and from the gods by virtue of their mortality. Their ability to speak and their culture or their skills at producing food and other goods separated them from animals and from supernatural beings— centaurs, cyclopes, sirens, and other imaginary, nonhuman beasts— that dwelled on the margins of the world. The poems drew no great distinctions between Greeks and their neighbors who spoke non-Greek languages. Several centuries later, Thucydides reaffirmed that the customs of the early Greeks were, in fact, not so different from those of neighboring communities, and that customs differentiating them in the latter part of the fifth century b.c. were recent developments.[8]

The world depicted in the *Iliad* and *Odyssey* was rapidly transformed in the late sixth century b.c., after the Persian Empire had sacked Nineveh, the Neo-Assyrian capital, destroyed the Neo-Babylonian empire, and started to threaten the Greek-speaking communities of Asia Minor and the Aegean. The latter responded to the Persian threat in various ways. By 500 b.c., for instance, the local communities of

Attica had forged a cross-class alliance, which laid the foundations for the democratic, non-dynastic Athenian polis. All of the men from the local communities, regardless of their status, became citizens of Athens. Their identities were defined by their citizenship and by virtue of their being neither foreigners nor women. With the power and solidarity of the local communities appropriated by the Athenian state and the roles of traditional leaders usurped by tyrants like the mythic Oedipus, the distinctions between men, foreigners, and women were recast in increasingly hierarchical terms.[9]

The Greeks, using their impressions of the Persians as a model, invented the idea of the barbarian during the first half of the fifth century b.c. Members of the Persian court lived in luxury and did not speak Greek, they declared, and the Persian ruler was a despot. Barbarians were emotional, cruel, dangerous, polygamous and incestuous; some even practiced human sacrifice.[10] Most importantly, barbarians did not live in democratic city-states; they were, in a word, the antithesis of the Greeks. Barbarians, thus characterized, quickly became familiar figures in the Greek city-states, especially since they were vividly portrayed in the tragedies and comedies of ruling-class playwrights such as Aeschylus and Sophocles, whose works were performed each year before large crowds.[11]

New hierarchically organized gender relations also emerged in Athens during the fifth century as the traditional male leaders of the local communities sought to retain their authority and maintain the integrity of the community against the incursions of the state. These leaders began to assert greater control over the marriage of their daughters. A father would promise his daughter to a man of higher status, which would enhance her kinsmen's position and possibly wealth as well as preserve their community. As the autonomy and choice of a woman declined, she would be married off as a child or adolescent by her father and would remain secluded in her husband's home to produce children for his family. When women protested their exclusion and attempted to assert their traditional rights, the play-wrights dismissed them as disloyal, emotional, irrational, or danger-ous. In a word, they claimed that the Athenian women were acting like barbarians who threatened to destroy the pillars of civilization.[12]

For example, in the *Oresteia*, Aeschylus describes Clytemnestra's challenge to her father's authority in particular and men's authority in general, when she murdered her husband on their wedding night, when she subsequently assumed his position as tyrant, and when she defeated men in verbal exchanges. In the Oedipus cycle, Sophocles described the marriage of an elite woman to a man of lower status and the threat her son, Oedipus, posed to traditional authorities and the established moral order. Euripides portrayed Medea—barbarian prin-cess, sorcerer, and murderer—as a dangerous animal who threatened to destroy family, polis, and culture.[13]

Greek writers did not have a monolithic view of barbarians in the latter half of the fifth century b.c., nor did they always portray them in an unfavorable light. Herodotus—a Persian subject from Halicar-nassus, a cosmopolitan Greek city in Asia Minor—described customs that distinguished Persians, Egyptians, Lydians, and other foreigners in his *History*. Euripides used the stereotype of barbarians as cowardly, treacherous, mean, uncultured, and morally inferior individuals to comment on Greek society. In *Troades* and *The Trojan Women,* he inverted the traditional hierarchy, which proclaimed the moral supe-riority of the Greeks and inferiority of the barbarians, to argue to his Athenian audiences that even Greeks behaved like barbarians on occasion. In these instances, the Greeks likened to barbarians and criticized for their behavior were not citizens of Athens; they came instead from city-states, like Thebes, that were fighting against Athe-nians in the Peloponnesian War.[14]

By the mid-fourth century b.c., democratic Athens was perhaps the major slave-owning state in the eastern Mediterranean. The demo-cratic institutions and practices were for the benefit of its literate citizen-soldiers. Their status placed these male citizens at the center of everyday life, where they were surrounded by foreigners, slaves, and women. Plato, an aristocrat from a family whose fortunes declined with the rise of Athenian democracy, was critical of democracy. In *The Republic*, he argued that men who were forced by economic circumstances to engage in productive labor should not be permitted to rule or even to enjoy citizenship. These rights, he contended, should be restricted to those trained in politics—that is, those who had the resources and time to devote themselves to learning the technical skills required to hold office and rule.[15]

A generation later, Aristotle expressed fear of diversity in his *Politics*. The aristocratic tutor of Alexander the Great, Aristotle informed the citizens of the Greek city-states that barbarians—typically pastoralists or brigands rather than farmers—were, by their very nature, ideal candidates for slavery. He also explained that women should be controlled, since the rights retained by the women of Sparta were ultimately responsible for the deplorable culture and downfall of that state.[16] Citizens occupied the highest rung in the social hierarchy of Athens, while aliens, women, slaves, and animals occupied subordinate positions on the social ladder.

The Hellenistic Greek and Roman writers who followed Aristotle also had well-developed views about the differences between civilized people and barbarians. The Roman writer Livy claimed barbarians were, by nature, enemies of the state. Cicero, the Roman orator and politician, portrayed the struggle between civilization and barbarism as a clash of manners and morals. Cicero also extended the idea of barbarism to the urban workers or plebeians who did not participate in politics. The patrician ruling class of Rome viewed the plebeians as rabble—uncivilized, ignorant, and violent. Cicero considered them to be as alien as barbarians, except that they were distant kin and neighbors who had been subordinated by the creation of the state. In his mind, both were examples of "the retarded, disoriented, irrational infancy of mankind, before man had begun to achieve better things for himself through his submission to law and the exercise of reason."[17] These indigenous barbarians were driven by irrational fury, lust, and self-delusion; they were either unable or unwilling to submit to civil and natural law, good morals, or the rule of reason. As a result, they stood at the opposite end of the spectrum from civilized patrician men. Tacitus, in contrast, preached to the Roman citizenry by describing the customs of German barbarians. In *Germania*, he praised the Germans for maintaining values the Romans had once possessed but now ignored or neglected.

Although St. Paul and other early Christian writers ignored the old boundaries between civilized societies and barbarian peoples, the Roman Christians changed their minds in the fourth century, after Christianity became the official state cult and its goals merged with those of the state. The cosmopolitanism of their predecessors was replaced by ethnocentrism and uncritical acceptance of a public culture promoted by the empire.[18]

RECOVERING OLD IDEAS ABOUT UNCIVILIZED PEOPLES IN THE RENAISSANCE

During the fourteenth and fifteenth centuries, commerce in the Mediterranean world was transformed, and the region's distribution of wealth and political power changed with it. Historical scholarship enjoyed a resurgence in both Mediterranean North Africa and Europe, as thinkers struggled to explain what had happened to their traditional social order.[19] Ibn Khaldn, a North African diplomat and civil servant, tied the social and cultural transformations of the late fourteenth century to changes in mercantile trade and the structures of everyday life.[20] From the fourteenth century onward, clerics, curial officials, judges, politicians, and merchants schooled in humanist thought at all-male universities and ecclesiastical academies began to study ancient texts and monuments in Rome, Padua, Verona, and the other city-states of northern Italy.[21] The new worldviews they constructed incorporated elements of classical and Judeo-Christian perspectives that were already widely known as well as other elements that they found buried away in the copyist archives of medieval monasteries. From the humanist standpoint, the new social order was dynamic, constantly in flux. Men could begin to regain the freedom lost during the Middle Ages by retrieving and developing the capacities possessed by the peoples of ancient Greece and Rome.

In addition to serving as standards of excellence and objects worthy of study and emulation, the authorities of classical antiquity also became a font of ideas about civilization and uncivilized peoples. Thus, on the eve of the transatlantic expansion of the late 1400s, the civilized classes of Europe acquired a rich new vocabulary to describe the uncivilized they encountered. *Barbarians* were treacherous, cruel, illiterate, uncultured foreigners with different languages and customs. *Pagans* were rustics who remained non-Christian idolaters even after Christianity had been adopted in the imperial cities. *Heathens* were polytheists—that is, they were neither Christian, Jew, nor Muslim. *Infidels* were those who adhered to religions—usually, but not exclusively, Islam—that Christians viewed as opposed to their own. *Savages* were wild, fierce, and cruel; ungovernable, devoid of culture, and neglectful of good behavior. They merged with another category, the *wild men*. These hairy individuals had fallen from human status and lived in the wilderness like animals, avoiding human beings and relying on strength and aggressive actions to survive. They lacked both the ability to speak and the capacity to conceive of God.[22]

The civilized classes of Europe distinguished themselves from others by combining these categories in various ways. Tartars might be barbarians and heathens; Berbers from the Barbary Coast could be barbarians and infidels. Gerald of Wales, a twelfth-century Anglo-Welsh

servant of the English king, discovered a resemblance between the
Irish Christians, whose homelands had recently been invaded and
settled by the English, and the barbarian societies described by Classical writers. In an unflattering and unfavorable assessment of Irish
society, he noted:

> This people is a sylvan folk, inhospitable; a people subsisting on cattle only
> and living bestially; a people who have not departed from the primitive
> pastoral life. Mankind generally progresses from the forests to the fields
> and thence to the towns and the conditions of citizens; but this nation,
> despising agricultural labor, not coveting the riches of cities, and averse to
> civil laws, follows the same life as their forefathers in forests and open
> pastures, willing neither to abandon old habits or learn anything new.[23]

The difficulties these Irish barbarians posed for the English Crown
included resistance to both taxation and control.

THE SLAVE TRADE

Changes in the medieval slave trade brought peoples from new parts
of the world to Western Europe. From the late thirteenth to the
mid-fifteenth century, merchants from Genoa had purchased captives
from Scandinavia and Slavs from Russia and the Balkans in Black Sea
slave markets located in the Crimea and near the mouth of the Don
River. By 1400, these peoples probably constituted a majority of
Europe's slaves. However, after the Turks conquered Constantinople
in 1453, West European slave dealers lost their access to the Black Sea
markets. From the mid-fifteenth century onward, the importance of
Genoan and Venetian slave merchants diminished as Castile and
Portugal struggled for hegemony over the Guinea coast of Africa and
gradually introduced a new, largely African, slave population in Lisbon,
Valencia, and Seville. As early as 1460, a Lisbon decree distinguishing
between "black and white slaves" partly recognized the diverse origins

emerging in the local slave community, although it did not accurately represent this diversity.[24]

By the 1490s the slave population of Iberian Peninsula became even more diverse. Large numbers of Jews and Muslims were captured and enslaved during the reconquest of the peninsula by the Christian states. They were joined in the slave markets of Lisbon and Seville by several thousand Native Americans brought in by Christopher Columbus, probably the decade's largest slave dealer. Columbus justified his actions by claiming that the enslaved Indians were war captives who had opposed his activities; worse yet, they were cannibals.[25]

Castilian merchants engaged in the nascent African slave trade were unhappy with the competition posed by Columbus and fearful that they would be excluded from the potentially lucrative Indies market. Together with theologians, the merchants won a decree from Queen Isabella in the year 1500 prohibiting the enslavement of American Indians. Just three years later, the Indies merchants were able to persuade the queen to rescind the ban. They were once again free to capture and enslave Indian men, women, and children whom they deemed to be cannibals. Yet only two years after that, in 1505, the first shipment of African slaves arrived in the Indies. This signaled a victory for the Queen, for clergymen who opposed the enslavement of Indians on theological grounds, and for the Castilian slave traders who were purchasing war captives along the African coast. The Crown gained revenues from the import licenses required for slaves coming from outside the Indies. The African slave merchants gained access to the American market. Theologians were able to lay the foundations for applying Aristotle's notion of natural slavery to the American Indians—an argument, as we saw in chapter 3, that they would make repeatedly for the next fifty years.[26]

NATIVE AMERICANS AND THE FORMATION
OF COLONIAL SOCIETY

First-generation Spaniards attempted to legitimate their domination of Native Americans with Aristotle's argument about natural
slavery. In the process of conquest, they homogenized highly diverse
indigenous communities, assigning them to the *república de indios*. In
areas such as Mexico and Peru where class-stratified states already
existed, Indian commoners were compelled to pay labor taxes and
tribute in kind to a small number of Spaniards and a few native nobles
who were granted encomiendas in the years immediately following the
invasion. In exchange, the commoners received religion and civilization. Legally defined as free vassals of the Spanish crown, they could
not enter into legal contracts without the approval of their guardian.[27]

Colonial authorities were particularly concerned with the legal
status and fiscal obligations of *Mestizos,* unions between colonizer and
colonized. The treatment of Mestizos varied considerably, reflecting
differences in their status and wealth, the identities of their parents,
and whether their parents were legally married. Mestizos who acquired
Indian lands through purchase or dowry could maintain their estates,
travel freely, bear arms, and enter religious orders. Those who were
"illegitimate" or whose origins were obscure or unknown were viewed
with more suspicion. They were barred from office and certain
occupations and shut off from the wealth and tribute of the native
communities. On the other hand, they were exempt from labor tax
and tribute obligations.

The Mestizos lived mainly in urban and mining centers. Some were
small farmers, merchants, or shopkeepers; those who were marginally
employed supported themselves through temporary labor, begging,
gambling, theft, prostitution, and banditry. This portrait also applies
to more than half of the Spaniards who resided in the colonies in the

1550s and the untold thousands of Indians who, for one reason or another, left their natal communities or were separated from them.[28] In colonial Latin American society, status was not fixed and immutable. One avenue of social mobility open to very wealthy non-noble Indians, Mestizos, and blacks was the purchase of *certificados de limpieza de sangre* (certificates of purity of blood) from the Church. These seventeenth- and eighteenth-century documents confirmed that the buyers were the "pure-blooded" descendants of old Spanish Christian families and that none of their ancestors were Jews, Moors, or heretics. Indians seeking social mobility could leave their natal community. While complaining about the difficulty of collecting labor taxes and tribute, a Spanish colonial official in southern Peru during the 1730s remarked that "the Indian cannot be distinguished from the Spaniard by the configuration of his features." He claimed that the racial categories of the colony were, in fact, socioeconomic categories and observed that "if an Indian cut his hair, entered into the service of a Spaniard, changed his dress and learned Spanish, he became indistinguishable from a Mestizo, and if he learned a profession, his descendants could pass as Mestizos or even Spaniards."[29]

These quasi-racial social categories—Spaniard, Indian, Negro, and Mestizo—were developed and sustained by state institutions and practices as integral parts of the conquest of the Iberian Peninsula and the New World; they were invented as the relationship between the colonizer and the colonized formed and evolved. Consequently, what they signified was contested, varied, and, at times, ambiguous.

An individual's identity and place in the colonial social structures of eighteenth-century Latin America were not based on the presence or absence of some essential feature in his or her physical appearance. They were determined by a complex interplay of various institutions, conditions, and practices, including socially constructed and reproduced heritages; degree of integration into a particular polity; class position; and participation in groups and activities, such as the religious festivals of the *cofradías* (Catholic lay associations), that proclaimed and reaffirmed membership and affiliation. The continuous interplay of these and other relations shaped and gave meaning to everyday life. They became the terrain of domination, exploitation, and oppression; they were the arenas of conflict and resistance. Within these arenas, the class struggles and culture wars of Spain's colonial empire were fought with the weapons of popular culture—music, dance, esthetics, and fiestas.[30]

SAVAGES, BARBARIANS, AND CIVILIZED PEOPLES

By the late 1500s, the diversity of human societies was beginning to be understood in terms of a hierarchy of types, capped by Western European civilization. As we saw in chapter 2, the Spanish Jesuit José de Acosta—a high Church official in colonial Peru and the Spanish king's representative to the Pope—suggested a distinction between savages and barbarians in the 1580s: Savages lacked law, government, and permanent places of residence; barbarians had governments and fixed places of residence but were uncultured and illiterate. This hierarchy of social types gave meaning to the cultural variety that the colonizers observed in the Americas. Even if the Aztec and Inca states bore some resemblance to Western European civilization, in this hierarchy their inhabitants were nonetheless considered barbarians who lacked an alphabet and spoke languages that could not deal with the subtleties of Christianity. Hence, imposing this hierarchy to subordinate these "barbarian" states was accomplished with relative ease by the Europeans. At the same time, the settlers encountered difficulties in attempting to dominate "savage" communities such as the Tupinamba of Brazil in which custom and egalitarian social relations prevailed, rather than law and formal governmental structures.

By 1777, when William Robertson wrote *The History of America,* this hierarchy of social types—savage, barbarian, and civilized—had assumed a temporalized form. Human social development was portrayed as a progression from savagery to barbarism to civilization. The institutions and practices concerned with subsistence were considered the most important; they played an important role in shaping all the others. Savage peoples fished and hunted, according to the schema of Robertson and his contemporaries in Scotland; they lived in small communities and were characterized by a sense of independence, attachment to community, and satisfaction with their own condition and circumstances. They had little idea of property and possessed no viable form of government, because their sense of subordination was imperfect. They also displayed no evidence of speculative reasoning or the use of abstract ideas.[31]

In the New World, Robertson asserted, only the peoples of Mexico and Peru had progressed toward civilization. However, their great empires, though considerably more advanced than the small independent tribes of savages that surrounded them, remained barbarous. While acknowledging that they farmed, he believed (incorrectly) that they had acquired domesticated animals and metallurgy quite late and therefore their progress toward civilization was retarded. Civilized peoples had a number of characteristics that differentiated them from savages and barbarians: cities, social classes, state institutions and practices, commerce, writing, and continuous wars. However, the most important feature separating civilized societies from the lower forms was their belief in the right to private property.

CROWDS, THE MASSES, AND DANGEROUS CLASSES

Christianity and other cosmopolitan or universalizing worldviews, while asserting the moral or spiritual unity of humanity, have never completely bridged the chasm separating civilized people from barbarians.

Crises are an integral feature of civilizations, and they provoke rulers and their agents to recycle negative images or to invent new forms of difference to legitimatize subordination and oppression. Rather than be restrained by cosmopolitan and universalizing philosophies, they appropriate these philosophies to buttress the stereotypes they have resurrected or created. In other words, they portray the members of subordinated classes or peasantries as barbarians and depict their inferiority as a consequence of unchanging essences that are rooted either in nature or human nature rather than deliberate human acts.

For example, Edmund Burke, a conservative critic of the French Revolution, denounced the participants in the 1789 uprising who came together outside of state institutions and in opposition to them, as a "swinish multitude"—a rabble composed of the most undesirable elements of society. These "dregs of society"—whom he described as "bandits," "savages," "street-prowlers," "beggars," and "prostitutes," became a "band of cruel ruffians and assassins [and] ... the vilest of women."[32] This crowd, he declared, was an angry, violent mob driven by criminal instincts and by irrational, insatiable desires to loot, to destroy property, to consume alcoholic beverages, and to inflict bodily harm on innocent citizens. Its pathological behavior revealed the dark side of human nature.

In the 1870s, in the aftermath of the Franco-Prussian War and the destruction of the Paris Commune, the French social critic and popularizer of science Gustave Le Bon resurrected and embroidered Burke's denunciation of the masses. Le Bon asserted that the evolutionary progression of social types from savage to barbarian to civilized also reflected changes in intelligence. He measured the heads of several hundred men and women and declared that the results supported his theory.

Western Europeans, Le Bon claimed, were more intelligent than modern savages—i.e., the tribal peoples of the Americas and Africa;

*A common depiction of the French Revolution as the destruction of
a noble aristocracy by loutish, brutal rabble. [Culver Pictures, Inc.]*

men were more intelligent than women—whose brains had shrunk
as their activities were increasingly restricted to the domestic sphere;
and scientists and industrialists were more intelligent than peasants,
factory workers, and servants—that is, the barbarous classes of civilized society. He then asserted that the succession of cranial capacities—brain size—beginning with children at the low end of the scale,
and progressing through savages, women, and workers, to the high
levels of scientists, provided empirical proof of the stages through
which human intelligence had evolved. He also asserted that criminals
had a distinctive shape to their skulls, showing they must be born with
hereditary mental conditions predisposing them to pathological behavior. These negative hereditary conditions and behaviors were, of
course, most commonly found among savages, women, and workers.[33]

Le Bon used his claims about intelligence to underscore several arguments in his influential *Psychology of Crowds* (1895). When individuals formed a crowd, he argued, they lost both their intellectual capacities and their individuality. Once their intellectual capacities were diminished, they were no longer able to distinguish what was real from what was imaginary. Unconscious elements surged up from the deep recesses of their minds, propelling them toward the "evil sentiments ... the atavistic residue of the instincts of primitive man."[34] The ideas and sentiments that unified participants in a crowd were contagious and spread by unconscious, involuntary processes of imitation. Moreover, claimed Le Bon, the special characteristics of crowds— their impulsiveness, irrationality, inability to reason, lack of judgment and critical perspective, and exaggeration of sentiments—were also evident in the "inferior forms" of human evolution (women, for instance) who will always respect the will and wishes of strong, forceful male leaders.

While Le Bon made a distinction between the behavior of crowds and the behavior of individual criminals, many of his contemporaries in Europe and the United States did not. In 1877, for instance, the editors of *Harper's Weekly* described participants in the Great Railroad Strike as barbarians who attacked property and massacred innocent people; on the same page, they portrayed the Nez Perce Indians as a criminal class that made war on civilization itself.[35]

Le Bon's claims echoed the efforts of Cesare Lombroso to identify anatomical features that were distinctive in criminals and the insane. After considerable research, Lombroso announced that the high cheek bones, handle-shaped ears, and large jaws found in skulls of criminals, savages, and apes correlated with their common behavioral characteristics: idleness, insensitivity, ferocity, and love of tattoos, enabling him to identify "born criminals."

For Lombroso, criminality was both natural and unacceptable. His studies were, and still are, used by the state to underwrite policies calling for detention, differential sentencing, capital punishment, and control of reproduction. Not surprisingly, the markers of hereditary criminality and insanity were much more common in the lower classes from the backward, more primitive parts of Southern Italy than among the middle classes from the civilized North.[36]

Lombroso's views persist to this day, if somewhat toned down and modified. In 1937, Harvard anthropologist Earnest Hooton observed that criminal types were more round-headed than civilized people, and that "we must abandon hope of sociological palliatives and face the necessity of dealing with [these hereditary] biological realities."[37] More recently, in yet another echo of Lombroso, the following claim was made in 1965 and recycled sporadically ever since: That "males with an extra Y chromosome exhibit criminal tendencies (they are XYY rather than the 'normal' XY) ...[and] that XYY males are present with higher than expected frequency in an institution for the criminally insane in Scotland."[38] The danger, of course, with claims like these— buttressed with allegedly scientific evidence—is that they are quickly adopted to justify discriminatory political policies and practices.

SEXUAL DIFFERENCES, GENDER, AND SEXISM

The rise of civilization has always had different consequences for the men and women of the producing classes and their counterparts in the elite, nonproducing groups associated with the state. In the process, the power, authority, and status of women in both classes have typically eroded, but in different ways. At one level, the changes have involved the reorganization of labor processes. When a portion of the work of producing-class women has been transformed into labor or tribute appropriated by the state, elite women have withdrawn from production. At another level, it has involved the reorganization of the politics of everyday life. While elite women were gradually squeezed out of the emerging public sphere of social life, women (and men) of the producing classes never had access to this sphere from the time it was being organized.[39]

This kind of transformation and exclusion occurred in the wake of the French Revolution. Although many women were active participants in the revolution, when the specter of war with England and Spain loomed on the horizon, only property-owning men residing in France gained the right of citizenship. In addition, the barriers that had prevented women from participating in politics remained in place. By 1793, the National Convention decided that even women owning property could not exercise political rights or take an active role in government. Over the next two years, women's political clubs were outlawed; women were prohibited from attending meetings of the Convention unless they were accompanied by a male citizen; and groups of more than five women found in public were legally subject to dispersion by force.[40]

Needless to say, the processes by which women have been excluded from the public arenas of civilization have always been rooted in historically contingent social relations. Enlightenment scientists and physicians, in their quest to discover universally valid laws, sought empirical evidence that would show that there were natural differences between the male and female of the human species and, hence, between men and women. This effort compelled these scientists to reject the beliefs of earlier writers who had asserted that the differences between men and women were mainly political.

Classical writers generally claimed that the boundary between men and women was one of degree rather than kind. Aristotle, for instance, believed that there were no sexual differences between men and women—that the two genders (men and women) corresponded to a single sex. Men—that is, biological males—were the norm, and women (biological females) were imperfect men, errors of nature that deviated from the norm. The organs of deviants—that is, women— were the same, but hidden inside their bodies.[41] This unnatural distortion had several consequences, Aristotle declared: Women were passive; they necessarily occupied a lower rung of the social ladder than citizens who were, by definition, normal (biological males). These citizens—that is, men who participated in the politics of the city-state—were the active agents of culture. The only women depicted in Aristotle's writings were the wives and daughters of citizens, whose place in civil society was ultimately validated by their relation to particular men. They resembled slaves, who lacked gender attributes and whose place in the polis also reflected their subordination and the services they provided to citizens and the state.[42]

Even as they rejected the single-sex model, John Locke and Jean Jacques Rousseau—who did much to lay the foundations for liberal and romantic social thought, respectively—adopted Aristotle's view that men were active agents and women were passive. Locke claimed that the man ruled the family by virtue of his greater strength and intellectual capacity. In *Emile* (1760), Rousseau cataloged the physical characteristics that distinguished men from women and then listed the moral differences that they engendered. Due to these differences, men and women should not be educated in the same manner. Moreover, he argued, because these biologically rooted differences were actually complementary in the family, the man was destined to be strong and the woman passive.[43]

By 1800, most of the Enlightenment commentators on sex had already dismissed the single-sex model favored by classical and medieval writers. They effectively turned Aristotle upside down, claiming that there were fundamental differences between the male and female sexes, and hence between men and women. These sexual distinctions were of kind, not degree; they were rooted in the anatomical and biological differences observed by anatomists and naturalists. This implied that the relations between men and women also involved a series of contrasts rather than gradations.[44]

More importantly, in their view, a person's destiny was ultimately shaped by her or his anatomy. However, by adopting this view, the Enlightenment scientists and their successors failed to appreciate sufficiently that human beings experience and determine the significance of sexual differences in cultural terms—that is, gender. Commentators who equate sexual (biological) differences with gender (cultural) differences overlook the fact that members of different societies do not necessarily understand the relationship of *male* to *man* and *female* to *woman* in the same way. Gender relations, and other relations as well, are historically and culturally contingent. These theorists also fail to acknowledge that their own constructions and understandings of both sexual difference and of gender were radically transformed toward the end of the eighteenth century.

RACE AND RACISM

Some of the Enlightenment scientists who wrote about sex and gender differences also devised classifications of people based on their physical appearance and behavior. In 1684, a French physician, François Bernier, who was an acquaintance of John Locke, divided the peoples he had seen in the course of his travels into four groups based on skin color, stature, hair, and the shape of their nose and lips. Europeans, Hindus, and American Indians had a skin color that was accidental, the result of exposure to the sun; the color or Africans was essential; Asians had broad shoulders and flat faces; Lapps were "vile animals."[45] Bernier did not use this classification to construct either a hierarchy of human types or a genealogy of human history.

John Locke, as a colonial administrator, organic intellectual of emergent capitalism, and founding stockholder in the slave-trading Royal African Company, had no wish to challenge exploitation and the social hierarchy. He did, however, shift the rationale for dehumanizing and objectifying enslaved human beings from the innate characteristics of Aristotle's natural slavery to the doctrine of nominal essences. For Locke, every object had a real essence that was unknowable; however, that object also had observable attributes that could be compiled to represent its nominal essence. As a result, Locke and his successors could select a single trait—skin color, for example—from a list of characteristics and proclaim that it was the primary criterion defining humanity. Of course, scientists could and did disagree on which traits were essential. What Locke established was a logic for answering the question—a logic whose validity went largely unchallenged.[46]

The naturalists Carolus Linnaeus and Johann Blumenbach constructed the best known eighteenth-century taxonomies of race. In 1735, Linnaeus distinguished four races on the basis of moral, cultural, and physical criteria: their physical appearance, demeanor, how they covered their bodies, and whether they were governed by custom, opinion, or caprice. He described American Indians, Europeans, Asians, and Africans and arranged them in a hierarchy, with American Indians at the top, followed by Europeans, Asians, and Africans.[47]

In 1775, Blumenbach identified five races belonging to a single human species: Caucasian, Ethiopian, Mongolian, American Indian, and Malay. In his scheme, Caucasians were the original type; Malays and Ethiopians diverged in one direction and American Indians and Mongolians in another. Blumenbach also argued that there was a correspondence between intelligence and the size and shape of the head—a view that would become particularly influential in the nineteenth century.[48]

The discussions of race that emerged in the nineteenth century were shaped by commentators who viewed the Americas before the arrival of Europeans as either empty (Locke) or populated by peoples who, by virtue of their cultural practices, were savages (Robertson). In the United States, these discussions were also fueled by immigration, slavery, forced resettlement, the Haitian Revolution, and imperialist expansion carried out under the ideology of Manifest Destiny.

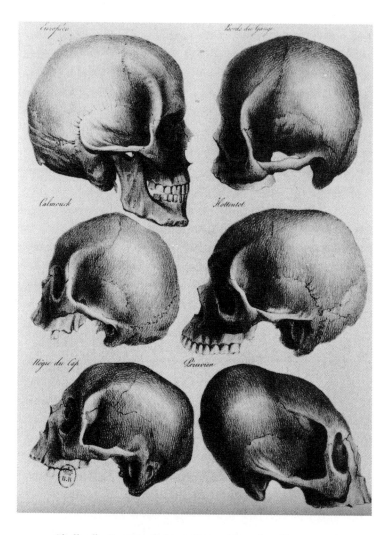

*Skull collection intended to portray a hierarchy of human races,
with the European at the top and the "Peruvian" closest to the animal.
[Bibliotheque Nationale (Paris, 1836).]*

Manifest Destiny as divine right enshrined racism and nativism, and made the seizure of territory from Texas to California through countless Indian wars and the 1846 war with Mexico seem like a religious crusade to tame the West.[49]

Discussions of race in the United States during the nineteenth century involved three intertwined strands. One, centered in the cultural and educational institutions of Philadelphia, sought to provide scientific validation for the existence of the racial hierarchies defined by Thomas Jefferson and other politicians. In the 1830s, Charles Caldwell, America's leading phrenologist, claimed that 1) the races of mankind—Caucasians, Mongolians, Indians, and Africans—were separate species, and 2) that, by virtue of being civilized, Caucasians stood at the top of the hierarchy. Nine years later, Samuel George Morton claimed that measurements he had made on 256 skulls showed that the average brain size of the five races defined by Blumenbach differed; in his view, Caucasians stood at the top of the hierarchy, for they had the largest skulls.[50]

The proponents of the second strand, emanating from Philadelphia and Harvard, attempted to show a linkage between race and health. In 1840s, they claimed the U.S. Census showed that the incidence of insanity was ten times higher among free blacks in the North than in the slave populations of the South. They also claimed that mulattos— that is, individuals with one black and one white birth parent—had higher mortality and shorter life expectancies than either of their parents. During the Civil War, the U.S. Sanitary Commission and the Provost Martial-General's Bureau—with advice from Harvard naturalist Louis Agassiz—measured nearly 24,000 soldiers, sailors, Indians, and prisoners of war to refine their understanding of racial types and their differences. The expenses of this project were underwritten in substantial part by nascent life insurance companies, whose statisticians used the data to establish the empirical foundations for differential premium and rate structures based on race.[51]

The third strand, also spawned at Harvard, proclaimed the racial superiority of Anglo-Saxon Protestants. This discovery was fueled by the arrival of a million Irish-Catholic immigrants between 1815 and 1845, westward expansion, and the inevitable collision with Mexico over territory. In 1843, Edward Everett, a Harvard professor and U.S. Ambassador to England, asserted the unsurpassed superiority of the Anglo-Saxon race. His Harvard colleagues—George Perkins Marsh, Henry Wadsworth Longfellow, George Bancroft, Francis Parkman, and William H. Prescott—concurred.

> They believed that the national character was largely a matter of race, that liberty was a special attribute of the Germanic/Anglo-Saxon peoples, and that Providence had directed human progress westward to America where the United States was engaged in the fulfillment of that plan.[52]

By the 1880s, the northern industrialists had already opened the doors of their new factories to immigrant laborers rather than Southern freedmen; in the process, social boundaries became more sharply demarcated. In 1890, anthropologist Daniel G. Brinton produced a new classification of races legitimating the common sense categories that were already used by the U.S. Census Bureau and that had prevailed in political debates for more than twenty years. The most distinctive feature of his classification was a set of "not quite white" races that separated Anglo-Saxons from darker-skinned subspecies. These buffer groups were the Eastern Europeans, Southern Europeans, and Semitic-Hamitic populations of the Iberian Peninsula, North Africa, and the Middle East.[53]

The census categories, buttressed by Brinton's racial hierarchy, had an important implication: that the emerging urban working class in the United States, primarily composed of immigrants, was not white but colored.[54] A decade later, William Z. Ripley used skull measurements to infer that the buffer races defined by the census and Brinton were less intelligent than whites from northern Europe. His views echoed those of the Immigration Restriction League, whose members lobbied Congress to stem the flow of immigrants from Eastern and Southern Europe.[55]

By the turn of the century, these theories provided a rich medium for the ideas of scientific racism, hereditary racial differences in intelligence, inherited criminality, and eugenics.[56] Through the census, the U.S. government was already keeping track of the birthplaces of members of immigrant communities as well as the birthplaces of their parents. In 1921, Congress finally enacted the legislation sought by the Immigration Restriction League. Activist scholars such as Franz Boas challenged the racism inherent in this legislation during the 1930s; however, the racial categories remained in place until World War II, when the U.S. government demonized the Japanese, incarcerated Japanese-Americans, and attempted to convince the members of the "not quite white" races that their primary identity was nationalist, white American. This turnabout was essential for building a military force composed overwhelmingly of conscripts in their late twenties.

The postwar payoff consisted of federally funded housing and the G.I. Bill, which provided 2.1 million men and 65,000 women with the financial resources to go to college. The beneficiaries were mostly white, reflecting the racial segregation of the time. Education became an avenue of social mobility for the offspring of immigrants from Southern and Eastern Europe; in the 1950 census, their ethnicity and place of birth, as well as the birthplaces of their parents, were no longer recorded. These changes transformed the "not quite white" ethnic buffer races of the 1930s into whites.[57]

Assimilation and integration were important political and social projects in the 1940s and 1950s. The validity of race as a biological category was denied in the 1952 UNESCO statement on race; one author, M.F. Ashley Montagu, argued that race was, in fact, a socially constructed category that provided an essential underpinning for racism.[58] Sociologists, such as Nathan Glazer and Daniel P. Moynihan, also downplayed the importance of race as a biological category, arguing instead for the importance of culture and ethnicity in the constitution of everyday life; they replaced race with the "culture of poverty" thesis which argued that the cultures of some ethnic groups were pathological, because their family structures were different from those who had achieved the benefits of the American Dream.

After the passage of the civil rights legislation of the mid-1960s, the language of social Darwinism, which had been muted but never silent, began to resurface with increasing vigor. A halt was called to the advances of the civil rights movement. The academy witnessed renewed interest in IQ studies and the debut of sociobiology. A rising argument in the field of ethnic studies contrasted the relative success of white immigrants to the declining conditions of communities of color, putting fault on the latter groups for alleged cultural deficiencies. Outside the academy, disproportionate numbers of young men of color, mostly in their late teens, were conscripted and served in Vietnam; on their return home, they received much less support than the beneficiaries of the G.I. Bill had gotten in the late 1940s.

During the past twenty-five years, the United States has experienced the second largest group of immigrants in its history. However, at the turn of the century, 95 percent of the immigrants came from Europe. Of the new arrivals, nearly 75 percent came from Asia or Latin America. The internal diversity of these immigrant communities, and a reorganization of U.S. class structure, have combined to promote "identity politics" and to create the conditions for a new racial hierarchy, with new buffer races and a recrudescence of racist violence. The latter was exacerbated by the Supreme Court's Bakke Decision in 1978 and President Reagan's cynical call for a "color-blind society" in the 1980s. More recent attacks on affirmative action in California, in 1995 at the University of California and in a 1996 ballot proposition, have revealed one of many facets of a resurgent racism. This is complemented by a return to the argument (once discredited among intellectuals) that racial differences rather than racism have laid the basis for social inequality.[60]

SUMMARY

In this chapter, we have examined some of the diverse categories of uncivilized people that have been invented and recycled by boosters of the concept of civilization to legitimatize social hierarchies and inequalities created by class and state formation. The ruling classes used these categories to distinguish themselves from subordinated classes and communities. In ancient Greece, political orators and playwrights initially invented the idea of the *barbarian* in response to the threat from the Persian state. They quickly extended this idea to include women, slaves, and even non-Athenian Greeks who were not behaving in ways deemed appropriate by ruling class men of Athens. The Roman ruling class extended the term *barbarian* even further to describe the customs and behavior of its own subordinated classes.

Much of the legitimacy these ideas enjoy today derives from their invention or use by historic authorities—such as the Scriptures, Aristotle, or John Locke—still regarded as relevant commentators for the present. Contemporary critics use the ideas and authority of earlier writers to construct genealogies for their own claims and to legitimate their views. Modern social critics, like their predecessors, also attempt to legitimatize the inequalities of class, gender, and racial oppression by claiming that socially constructed differences are, in reality, rooted in nature or in human nature. Difference is natural, they assert, so there is no point in attempting to remedy society's inequities. Many critics use these claims to support policies and practices that actually increase social inequalities.

UNCIVILIZED PEOPLES SPEAK

Civilization is a whole greater than the sum of its parts: a hierarchy of distinct classes, communities, and cultures linked together and organized by the institutions and practices of class and state structures. For the benefit of their ruling classes, civilizations have governments that maintain social order and laws that regulate relations between classes and ensure the availability and quality of commodities. Government and law shape the political and economic conditions of civilization, underwrite the growth of rational knowledge and economic development, and create conditions that nurture enlightenment and culture.

Ruling classes see themselves as the civilized classes. They cultivate beliefs, values, and goals that encourage the development and spread of what they perceive to be enlightened or refined behavior. The cultures they construct are distinctive and elite, with values and goals that they believe should be revered and emulated. These ruling classes, supported by the privileges they have appropriated for themselves, believe they possess the only true understanding of civilization. By

117

virtue of the polish and refinement they claim for themselves, these rulers see civilization standing in opposition both to nature and to the subordinated classes and communities, which they view as not civilized.

In the eyes of the ruling classes, these "uncivilized" groups are either a part of nature or a less developed, less perfect version of themselves. In the process of inventing uncivilized peoples, they typically blur or erase differences between peoples and at the same time create new categories. The label *Indian,* for example, is a ruling-class invention. Before the arrival of European settlers, Indians did not exist in the Americas. Rather, there were hundreds or thousands of indigenous communities whose members defined themselves as Abnaki or Sioux or Navaho or Taino. Some indigenous communities, such as the Seminoles, developed identities and cultural practices in the colonial encounter. In some cases, the same community was redefined, as happened with the Lumbee of North Carolina, who were legally reclassified from Indians to Free Persons of Color in the 1830s, and then back to Indians after 1865.[1]

This erasure or invention of difference has also characterized the approach of the ruling classes to African slaves who were brought to the Americas against their will and to the waves of immigrants from Ireland, the Mediterranean, Eastern Europe, and Asia who have occupied different layers of the U.S. working class. Not surprisingly, this class of non-indentured, wage-paid workers has been stratified by race and ethnicity since the nineteenth century.[2]

The behavior of members of ruling classes toward those whom they define and portray as uncivilized has tended to differ from the ways they consort with their own kind. The subordinated classes and communities have also seen other groups, especially the ruling elites, as different, and have acted accordingly toward them. Critics with views as divergent as those of Rousseau, Marx, and Nietzsche have remarked on this relationship, which the German philosopher Georg Wilhelm Friedrich Hegel called the master-slave relation.[3]

Europe Supported by Africa and America,
as depicted by William Blake (1792).

In *The Souls of Black Folk,* W.E.B. DuBois described the effects of barriers erected to separate whites and blacks in the 1890s and early 1900s:

> Now if one notices carefully one will see that between these two worlds, despite much physical contact and daily intermingling, there is almost no community of intellectual life or point of transference where the thoughts and feelings of one race can come into direct contact and sympathy with the thoughts and feelings of the other.[4]

The absence of a shared culture that crossed class and racial lines had important consequences, which DuBois termed "double consciousness":

It is a peculiar sensation, this double-consciousness, this sense of always looking at one's self through the eyes of others, of measuring one's soul by the tape of a world that looks on it in amused contempt and pity. One ever feels his twoness—an American, a Negro; two souls, two thoughts, two unreconciled strivings; two warring ideals in one dark body, whose dogged strength alone keeps it from being torn asunder.[5]

From this double life every American Negro must live, as a Negro and as an American, as swept on by the current of the nineteenth while struggling in the eddies of the fifteenth century—from this must arise a painful self-consciousness, an almost morbid sense of personality and a moral hesitancy which is fatal to self-confidence. The worlds within and without the Veil of Color are changing and changing rapidly, but not at the same rate, not in the same way; and this must produce a peculiar wrenching of the soul, a peculiar sense of doubt and bewilderment. Such a double life, with double thoughts, double duties, and double social classes, must give rise to double words and double ideals, and tempt the mind to pretense or revolt, to hypocrisy or radicalism.[6]

As a result of the master-slave relation, the uncivilized peoples invented during episodes of class and state formation typically had perceptions of civilization that differed from those of the rulers. Their subordinate locations in the structures of power as well as the events and circumstances of their everyday lives required them to examine civilization through different lenses from the rulers, and gave them a perspective distance that would allow them to forge and test alternative analyses. Since they were intimately acquainted with repression and resistance, they often recognized with great accuracy the exploitative nature of unequal power relations. They also have understood the structural reasons why their perspectives of civilization were both distinctive and opposed to those of the ruling classes and the state. One illustrative remark was transcribed from an antislavery meeting, where the former slave and Abolitionist leader Sojourner Truth responded to a speaker who had praised the U.S. Constitution:

Children, I talks to God and God talks to me. I go out and talks to God in de fields and de woods. I was walking out and I got over de fence. I saw de wheat a holding up its head, looking very big. I goes up and talks holt of it. You b'lieve it, dere was no wheat dere. I says, "God, what is de matter wit dis wheat?" and he says to me, "Sojourner, dere is a little weasel in it." Now I hears talkin' bout de Constitution and de rights of man. I come up and takes holt of dis Constitution. It looks mighty big, and I feel for my rights, but dere ain't any dere. Den I say, "God, what ails dis Constitution?" He says to me, "Sojourner, dere is a little weasel in it."[7]

Similarly, Chief Joseph wrote perceptively about the unequal power relations of civilization when he prescribed an alternative to the genocidal and ethnocidal practices of the U.S. government in the wake of the Nez Perce War in 1879:

I can not understand how the Government sends a man out to fight us, as it did General Miles, and then breaks his word. Such a Government has something wrong about it. I can not understand why so many chiefs are allowed to talk so many different ways, and promise so many different things.... I am tired of talk that comes to nothing.... There has been too much talking by men who had no right to talk. Too many misrepresentations have been made, too many misunderstandings have come up between the white men about the Indians. If the white man wants to live in peace with the Indian he can live in peace. There need be no trouble. Treat all men alike. Give them all the same law. Give them all an even chance to live and grow ... [since] all people should have equal rights....

I only ask of the Government to be treated as all other men are treated.... When I think of our condition my heart is heavy. I see men of my race treated as outlaws and driven from country to country, or shot down like animals....

We can not hold our own with the white men as we are. We only ask an even chance to live as other men live. We ask to be recognized as men. We ask that the same law shall work alike on all men....

Let me be a free man—free to travel, free to stop, free to work, free to trade where I choose, free to choose my own teachers, free to follow the religion of my fathers, free to think and talk and act for myself....[8]

The effects of the master-slave relation have called into question the truth of the civilized classes' constant assertion that they alone possess a true understanding of civilization. Since the 1750s, every time the implications of the master-slave relation have been raised, the civilized classes have either ignored them, denied their relevance, or attacked their validity. For example, when college curricula that attempted to incorporate multicultural perspectives came under attack, this was merely one of the more recent efforts to silence and erase the voices of subordinated classes and communities. This assault was launched in the late 1980s by conservative academics Allan Bloom, Lynn Cheney, and others who, like Roger Kimball (quoted in chapter 1), have sought to protect culture and civilization from the barbarians.[9] Their attack was buttressed in 1994 by the authors of *The Bell Curve* and their allies, who simply ignored the enormous body of twentieth-century research that challenges and undermines their claims of racially based levels of intelligence in the population.[10]

The multiculturalism controversy was just one example of the intellectual approach of ruling-class propagandists. When relating the circumstances surrounding challenges to their views, they have quickly passed over the fact that their own ideas were forged in the context of an argument. They sometimes have neglected even to mention that any objections to their views about the monolithic nature of civilization were ever raised. As a result, their revisionist accounts have recycled and renewed old arguments, but never the critiques of them. Thus they have tried to salvage the idea of civilization itself, as if it were something that transcends history and social relations.

Let us consider briefly a few of the ways in which the views and practices of the so-called uncivilized peoples regularly challenge the reality and validity of categories used by the ruling classes and the state to buttress their own legitimacy.

SUBVERTING THE RACIAL, ETHNIC, AND GENDER CATEGORIES OF THE STATE

Subordinated classes and communities often resist or reject the descriptive categories employed by the state. They disavow ascribed statuses and characteristics and substitute others that acknowledge the shared experiences of their everyday life, experiences that result from occupying a particular space and place in the class structure. By their very existence, Puerto Ricans in the United States and other national groups who construct their identity in historical terms confound the state's efforts to classify them in racial terms, as Angelo Falcón pointed out:

> Puerto Ricans presented an enigma to Americans because (from a North American perspective) Puerto Ricans were both an ethnic group and more than one racial group. Within the U.S. perspective, Puerto Ricans, racially speaking, belonged to both [white and black] groups; however, ethnically, they belonged to neither. Thus placed, Puerto Ricans soon found themselves caught between two polarities and dialectically at a distance from both. Puerto Ricans were White and Black; Puerto Ricans were neither White nor Black.[11]

In Chicago and other cities, the identities of street gangs organized around "turf" (bounded space) constitute another instance of resistance to the state's efforts to classify its population by race and ethnicity. Although gang members use labels that are also employed by the state, they infuse them with very different meanings. As Dwight Conquergood notes,

> Many of these street gangs originated during the 1960s and 1970s when much of Chicago was residentially segregated. The Latin Kings, the dominant

gang in my neighborhood ... originated in a section of the city farther south that was almost exclusively Puerto Rican.... As soon as neighborhoods became integrated, however, the local turf gangs became culturally diverse, even though they retained their ethnically-specific name. For example, my neighborhood, a port of entry for new immigrants, refugees and internally displaced migrants, is one of the ethnically most diverse in urban America: more than fifty languages and dialects are spoken at the local high school.... Correspondingly, the Latin Kings ... are Mexican Assyrian, African-American, Appalachian, Lebanese, Filipino, Palestinian, Greek, Panamanian, Salvadoran, Laotian, Korean, Vietnamese, and others—in addition to Puerto Rican. One of the vice-presidents of the Latin Kings was born in Iraq, and another one is a blond-haired freckled youth from Appalachia.[12]

In this way, the Latin Kings of Chicago and other gangs have shown a recognition of the completely artificial nature of the ethnic and racial statuses imposed on their members by the state in a context shaped by violence. By their understanding, these categories were not the product of some transcendental process rooted in human nature or biology, as the ruling classes, the state, and their agents have often suggested. Their alternative perspective on race and ethnicity was grounded in the creation and assertion of identity under circumstances shaped by domination, enforced inequality, and violence. It called into question both the legitimacy and the utility of hegemonic views that have emanated from the boosters of civilization.[13]

Subordinated peoples have sometimes succeeded in calling into question views that dominant classes hold about themselves. In one such instance, Ida B. Wells, the African-American journalist and political activist, brought lynching in the Southern United States to the attention of newspapers in England and to the white middle classes in the North.

After the Civil War, it was held in general by middle-class white men that American civilization was white, and that their own manliness depended on self-mastery and self-restraint. They further believed that African-Americans and the masses of Eastern and Southern

European immigrants were not civilized because their men lacked self-restraint. Turning this prejudice upside down, Wells argued that lynching was the uncivilized act of unmanly white male barbarians who lacked the self-restraint exhibited by African-American males in the South. Wells timed her anti-lynching campaign to coincide with the 1894 World Columbian Exposition in Chicago, which celebrated the march of American civilization. For the white middle classes in the North, as historian Gail Bederman pointed out, " 'Civilization' *naturalized* white male power by linking male dominance and white supremacy to human evolutionary development."[14] Wells's argument tore at the heart of this view and subverted the dominant understandings about the interconnections of race, civilization, and gender hierarchy. It marked the degeneration of American civilization toward a state of savagery. This carefully crafted argument jolted the white middle classes in the North out of their complacency and opened up the issue of racial violence.[15]

GENDER HIERARCHY IN A CONTEXT SHAPED BY RACE AND CLASS

Gender hierarchy is based on perceptions of how sex differences shape the social identities of men and women. Christine W. Gailey has referred to the way it describes "the association of social power with maleness; that is, with characteristics associated culturally with masculinity."[16] Since gender hierarchies have existed in all class-stratified societies, this form of oppression cross-cuts the forms resulting from class structures. In contemporary Western capitalist societies, patterns of behavior that are viewed as quintessentially male—such as competitiveness, playing golf, or the ideal of manly self-restraint that was manipulated so successfully by Ida Wells—are often identified with success, power, and the ability to control the actions of others.

Gender hierarchy ensures that men, by virtue of their gender, possess certain rights that women (and other genders) lack. Alva Belmont, a socially prominent matron of New York society and a suffragist, described its effects after witnessing the trials of union women who struck the Triangle Shirtwaist Company in 1909:

> Every woman who sits complacently amid the comforts of her home, or who moves with perfect ease and independence in her own protected social circle [by virtue of her class position], and says, "I have all the rights I want," should spend one night at the Jefferson Market Court. She would then know that there are other women who have no rights which man or law or society recognizes.[17]

More than eighty years ago, the novelist Mary Johnston captured the complex ways in which discourse on gender was shaped by class and race. In a letter to the president of the Equal Suffrage League of Virginia written in 1913, she said,

> I think as women we should be most prayerfully careful lest, in the future, women—whether coloured women or white women who are merely poor—should be able to say that we had betrayed their interests and excluded them from freedom.[18]

The civil and political rights of white women and of African-American men and women as a group were closely connected in the waning years of the Civil War. The wording of the Constitution's fourteenth amendment, which granted voting rights to African-American men who had been slaves before 1865, created a serious rift in the alliance of supporters of suffrage for both blacks as a group and women as a group. The rift deepened rapidly with the passage of the fifteenth amendment, which directed the federal government to provide aid for freedmen but not freedwomen. The controversy continued even after voting rights were extended to women by the passage of the nineteenth amendment in 1920.

The contours of the debates over civil and political rights were

complex. At times, racism threatened to divide the women's movement, or actually succeeded in dividing it, and gender inequalities tore
at heart of the black civil rights movement in an era increasingly shaped
by violence and repression. Sojourner Truth captured the pitfalls
created by the intersection of racism and gender hierarchy with great
precision in a passage stressing the urgency of universal suffrage for all
men and women:

> There is a great stir about colored men getting their rights, but not a word
> about the colored women; and if colored men get their rights, and not
> colored women theirs, you see the colored men will be masters over the
> women, and it will be just as bad as before. So I am for keeping the thing
> going while things are stirring; because if we wait till it is still, it will take
> a great while to get it going again.[19]

The members of the largely middle-class National Association of
Colored Women, founded in 1896 to fight lynching, tied progress to
the issue of the sexual exploitation of black women. According to
historian Deborah G. White, the association traced this exploitation
to the slavery era, "when white men used black women ... to reproduce
the slave population. When white men forbade legal slave marriages,
separated families, and took sexual advantage of slaves, they further
debased black women."[20]

They called for black men to show more support for black women
in their struggle against sexual exploitation. Association members,
including Ida B. Wells, believed that too many black men shared the
views of the dominant white society that black women lacked virtue.
Consequently, they confronted black ministers and others who cast
aspersions on the behavior, motives, and morality of black women,
demanding public apologies. In their view, noted White, "the sexual
exploitation of black women and oppression of black people were
connected."[21]

At the same time, they asserted their equality with black men, arguing that during slavery both had endured hardships and neither had gained anything positive. The association's Fannie Williams pointed out:

> In our development as a race, the colored woman and the colored man started even. The man cannot say that he is better educated and has had a wider sphere, for they both began school at the same time. They have suffered the same misfortunes. The limitations put upon their ambitions have been identical.[22]

Anna Cooper, another association member and the author of *A Voice from the South,* echoed Williams's views when she asserted that "gender equality grew from the denial of the franchise of race."[23] While such claims certainly created tensions between men and women, they did not deny black men an arena, nor did they challenge their predominance in the public sphere of the black community.

THE IMPORTANCE OF CLASS IN A CONTEXT SHAPED BY RACE AND GENDER

The issues of class and gender were explicitly linked by the middle-class women of the National Association of Colored Women, whose motto was "Lifting As We Climb." They believed they had a duty to provide services for poor and working black women and to educate them about the importance of leading a moral life. In their view, once poor and working black women adopted the manners and morality of the middle class, they would be more insulated from sexual exploitation and slander.[24] The subordination of women to the interests of capital was highlighted by Maggie Lena Walker, a Richmond, Virginia bank executive and community leader, in an address to the 1912 convention of the association:

Capital is deaf [as women rebel against unjust wages]—and will never hear their cries, until women force Capital to hear them at the ballot box, and to be just and honest to them as to the men.[25]

Three decades earlier, during the summer of 1881, more than 3,000 African-American washerwomen organized a strike in Atlanta to demand higher fees for their labor and to maintain control of their trade. At the time, Atlanta had the highest per capita number of domestic laborers of any city in the country. This was not the first time that domestic workers in the New South struck for better wages and for control over their working conditions. During the strike, the Atlanta City Council threatened to import "smart Yankee girls" to replace the local women and to levy a high business tax on every laundress in the city. In an open letter to the mayor, the women responded to the threat: " We have agreed, and are willing to pay $25 or $50 for licenses as a protection so we can control the washing for the city."[26]

This was not the first such strike in the South, and it was merely one tactic laundresses used to assert their autonomy, to express dissatisfaction with their employers, and to thwart efforts to exercise control over their lives. Others included quitting and creating the impression that labor was in scarce supply. These practices made it difficult for employers to replace workers or to find the ideal, suitably docile employee who would heed their every whim.

Class interests have often divided social movements based primarily on race and/or gender. The arguments in the 1920s over a proposed Equal Rights Amendment have remarkable resonance today. Many feminists supporting the amendment were middle-class women who sought access to universities and the professions. Their concept of equality was summed up by historians:

That anything other than strictly identical treatment of men and women was bound to be discriminatory; any use of the law to support gender distinctions would continue to deprive women of access to jobs, property, education, and more.[27]

Social feminists and working women in groups such as the Women's Trade Union League strongly opposed the amendment, arguing that

> some gender distinctions in law were necessary to protect women's health and safety in a most unequal world. For example, they feared that the ERA would be used by the courts to invalidate the protective labor legislation for which they had fought so hard—laws preventing employers from hiring women for heavy labor or night jobs....

> [Many] working women believed ... that poor women benefited more from the protective labor legislation than they would from an ERA. They believed that achieving substantive equality between men and women required recognizing and compensating for considerable social and economic inequalities. They were convinced that equal legal treatment on an unequal playing field would only create more inequality.[28]

Class issues were also evident in the emergence of black conservatism in the 1970s and 1980s. The decline of the U.S. economy, which began in the mid 1970s, had a greater impact on working class and poor African-Americans than it did on the first-generation black middle class, who were still able to pursue the educational, business, and political opportunities that had been opened by affirmative action programs. As Cornel West has noted, some members of the new black middle class

> began to feel uncomfortable about how their white middle-class peers viewed them.... The new black conservatives voiced these feelings in the form of attacks on affirmative actions programs (despite the fact that they had achieved their positions by means of these programs).

> The importance of this quest for middle-class respectability based on merit rather than politics cannot be overestimated in the new black conservatism. The need of black conservatives to gain the respect of their white peers deeply shapes certain elements of their conservatism. In this regard,

they simply want what most people want, to be judged by the quality of their skills, not the color of their skin....

The new black conservatives assume that without affirmative action programs, white Americans will make choices on merit rather than race. Yet they have adduced no evidence for this. Most Americans realize that job-hiring choices are made both on reasons of merit and on personal grounds. And it is this personal dimension that is often influenced by racist perceptions. Therefore the pertinent debates regarding black hiring is never "merit vs. race" but whether hiring decisions will be based on merit, influenced by race-bias against blacks, or on merit, but with special consideration for minorities and women, as mandated by law.[29]

The processes of class formation that have occurred in the United States since the 1970s have shaped the views of the new black conservatives in other ways, as has the desire for acceptance. Many African-Americans have identified with oppressed peoples in other parts of the world, such as Northern Ireland, South Korea, Poland, the Middle East, or South Africa. This internationalism, crystallized in civil rights and black power activism in the 1960s, has been based on a sense of shared social, political, and economic experiences. Eager to gain acceptance and avoid charges from the political right that they are "anti-American," the new black conservatives have rejected this internationalism and supported U.S. government policies in Central America, Israel, and Africa. As a result, they have often been attacked as "apologists" in their natal communities.[30]

CONCLUSIONS

The examples cited above illustrate instances in which subordinated classes and communities challenged efforts by the state and ruling classes to categorize and describe them. Each of the writers and activists quoted stripped away the veneer of civility and culture to expose the exploitation and oppression that underlie the hierarchical relations of civilized society. It would take very little effort to find dozens of other comments expressing the same sentiments with the same clarity of thought.

The ruling classes and their intellectual employees have repeatedly argued that the social and cultural hierarchies of civilized society are natural. Despite this, the members of subordinated classes and communities have proven to be amazingly cognizant of the fact that those hierarchies, as well as the categories on which they are based, are inventions that mask exploitative, oppressive social relations.

Thus, we need to think seriously about whose interests are served when we repeat claims that hierarchical social relations are inevitable or that oppressive social relations and violence are the immutable, natural outcome of history. We cannot continue to treat the idea of civilization uncritically. Assertions that civilization is desirable, beneficial, or superior to societies that lack similar hierarchical social relations merely perpetuate and promote the views of the powerful, self-proclaimed bearers and arbiters of culture and knowledge. Such assertions ultimately distort history. They trivialize the accomplishments of subordinated communities and classes and deny their members roles in making their own history. Recognizing the existence of subordinated groups, acknowledging their contributions and the historical roles they have played, and understanding their views about life ultimately challenges the validity of accounts that disregard them or deny them agency in shaping their own lives.

NOTES

CHAPTER 1: INVENTING CIVILIZATION

1. David Remick, "Lost in Space," *The New Yorker,* 5 December 1994, pp. 79-86.
2. Quoted in "Menace to Society," *Philadelphia Daily News,* 12 November 1994, p. 1.
3. Quoted in Catherine S. Mainegold, "Gingrich, Now a Giant, Aims at Great Society," *New York Times,* 12 November 1994, p. A11.
4. Quoted in Michael Posner, "Gingrich: English Must Rule," *Philadelphia Daily News,* 16 June 1995, p. 4.
5. Roger Kimball, " 'Tenured Radicals': A Postscript," *New Criterion* (January 1991): 13.
6. Richard J. Herrnstein and Charles Murray, *The Bell Curve: Intelligence and Class Structure in American Life* (New York: The Free Press, 1994), p. 288; see also Steven Fraser, ed., *The Bell Curve Wars: Race, Intelligence, and the Future of America* (New York: Basic Books, 1995).
7. Herrnstein and Murray, ibid., p. 543.
8. Michel J. Crozier, Samuel P. Huntington, and Joji Watanuki, *The Crisis of Democracy: Report on the Governability of Democracies to the Trilateral Commission* (New York: New York University Press, 1975), pp. 112-15, 161-64.
9. Samuel P. Huntington, *The Clash of Civilizations? The Debate* (New York: Council on Foreign Relations, 1993), p. 24.
10. Ibid., p. 25.

133

11. Ibid., p. 40.
12. Ibid., pp. 26-28.
13. Ibid., p. 44.
14. Ibid., p. 45.
15. Ibid., p. 49.
16. Ibid., p. 49.
17. See the essays collected in John Keane, ed., *Civil Society and the State: New European Perspectives* (London: Verso, 1988).
18. Yü Ying-shih, "Han Foreign Relations," in Denis Twitchett and Michael Loewe, eds., *The Cambridge History of China*, vol. 1: *The Ch'in and Han Empires, 221 B.C.—A.D. 220* (Cambridge, UK: Cambridge University Press, 1986), pp. 379-80.
19. Thomas C. Patterson, *The Inca Empire: The Formation and Disintegration of a Pre-Capitalist State* (Oxford: Berg Publishers, 1991).
20. Zia Sardar, Ashis Nandy, and Merryl W. Davies, *Barbaric Others: A Manifesto of Western Racism* (London: Pluto Press, 1993).
21. Pierre Clastres, *Society Against the State: Essays in Political Anthropology* (New York: Zone Books, 1987), pp. 189-218.
22. Martin Bernal, *Black Athena: The Afroasiatic Roots of Classical Civilization*, vol. 1, *The Fabrication of Ancient Greece 1785-1985* (London: Free Association Books, 1987); and Thomas C. Patterson, *Toward a Social History of Archaeology in the United States* (Ft. Worth, TX: Harcourt Brace, 1995), pp. 33-68.

CHAPTER 2: CIVILIZATION AND ITS BOOSTERS

1. See Perry Anderson, *Lineages of the Absolutist State* (London: New Left Books, 1974), pp. 15-59, 195-235; Victor G. Kiernan, *State and Society in Europe, 1550—1650* (Oxford: Basil Blackwell, 1980), pp. 1-19; A. D. Lublinskaya, *French Absolutism: The Crucial Phase, 1620-1629* (Cambridge, UK: Cambridge University Press, 1968), pp. 1-102; and, for similar processes in the Ottoman state, Rifa'at 'Ali Abou-El-Haj, *Formation of the Modern State: The Ottoman Empire, Sixteenth to Eighteenth Centuries* (Albany: State University of New York Press, 1991).
2. Rodney Hilton, *Class Conflict and the Crisis of Feudalism: Essays in Medieval Social History* (London: The Hambledon Press, 1985), pp. 239-45.
3. George Huppert, "The Idea of Civilization in the Sixteenth Century," in Anthony Molho and John A. Tedeschi, eds., *Renaissance Studies in Honor of Hans Baron* (DeKalb: Northern Illinois University Press, 1971), pp. 757-69; Lucien Febvre, " 'Civilization': Evolution of a Word and a Group

of Ideas," in Peter Burke, ed., *A New Kind of History, From the Writings of Lucien Febvre* (London: Routledge and Kegan Paul, 1973), pp. 219-57.
4. Alexander Murray, *Reason and Society in the Middle Ages* (Oxford: Clarendon Press, 1991), pp. 237-44.
5. Quoted by David B. Quinn, "Ireland and Sixteenth Century European Expansion," *Historical Studies* 1 (1958): 27.
6. Quoted by David B. Quinn, "Sir Thomas Smith (1513-1577) and the Beginnings of English Colonial Theory," *Proceedings of the American Philosophical Society* 89 (1945): 551. See also Nicholas P. Canny, "The Ideology of English Colonization: From Ireland to America," *The William and Mary Quarterly* 30 (1973): 575-98, and *Kingdom and Colony: Ireland in the Atlantic World, 1560—1800* (Baltimore: Johns Hopkins University Press, 1988).
7. John H. Rowe, "Ethnography and Ethnology in the Sixteenth Century, *Kroeber Anthropological Society Papers*, no. 30 (Spring 1964): 1-20; Sabine MacCormack, *Religion in the Andes: Vision and Imagination in Early Colonial Peru* (Princeton, NJ: Princeton University Press, 1991), pp. 266-67; and Anthony Pagden, *The Fall of Natural Man: The American Indian and the Origins of Comparative Ethnology* (Cambridge, UK: Cambridge University Press, 1982).
8. George Huppert, "The idea of Civilization,", p. 769; Samuel Kinser, "Ideas of Temporal Change and Cultural Process in France, 1470-1535," in Molho and Tedeschi, *Renaissance Studies*, pp. 705-55; John B. Bury, *The Idea of Progress: An Inquiry into Its Growth and Origin* (New York: The Macmillan Company, 1932); and Edgar Zilsel, "The Genesis of the Concept of Scientific Progress," in Philip J. Wiener and Aaron Noland, eds., *Roots of Scientific Thought: A Cultural Perspective* (New York: Basic Books, 1971), pp. 251-75.
9. Frederick J. Teggart, *The Idea of Progress: A Collection of Readings* (Berkeley: University of California Press, 1949), pp. 134-40.
10. John L. Brown, *The Methodus ad Facilem Historiarum Cognitionem of Jean Bodin: A Critical Study* (Washington, DC: Catholic University of America Press, 1939), pp. 86-119.
11. David Dickson, "Science and Political Hegemony in the 17th Century," *Radical Science Journal*, no. 8 (1979): 7-37; and Julian Martin, *Francis Bacon, The State, and The Reform of Natural Philosophy* (Cambridge, UK: Cambridge University Press, 1992).
12. Evelyn Fox Keller, *Reflections on Gender and Science* (New Haven, CT: Yale University Press, 1985), pp. 43-56; Val Plumwood, *Feminism and the Mastery of Nature* (London: Verso, 1993), pp. 108-109.
13. Art Berman, *Preface to Modernism* (Urbana: University of Illinois Press, 1994); Marshall Berman, *All That is Solid Melts into Air: The Experience*

of Modernity (New York: Penguin Books, 1988), pp. 16-23; Stephen Toulmin, *Cosmopolis: The Hidden Agenda of Modernity* (New York: The Free Press, 1990), pp. 5-89; Kathleen Okruhik, "Birth of a New Physics or Death of Nature," in Elizabeth D. Harvey and Kathleen Okruhik, eds., *Women and Reason* (Ann Arbor: University of Michigan Press, 1992), pp. 63-76.

14. Philip Abrams, "Notes on the Difficulty of Studying the State," *Journal of Historical Sociology* 1, no. 1 (1988): 75-78; see also Norbert Elias, *The Civilizing Process* (New York: Pantheon Books, 1982), 2 vols.

15. Thomas Hobbes, *Leviathan* (Harmondsworth, UK: Penguin Books, 1968), ch. 13; see also C.B. MacPherson, *The Theory of Possessive Individualism: Hobbes to Locke* (Oxford: Oxford University Press, 1962), and Ronald Meek, *Social Science and the Ignoble Savage* (Cambridge, UK: Cambridge University Press, 1976), pp. 17-23.

16. John Locke, *Second Treatise of Government* (Indianapolis, IN: Hackett Publishing Co., 1980), pp. 8-65.

17. John Locke, *Thoughts Concerning Education* (1694); see also James L. Axtell, *The Educational Writings of John Locke* (Cambridge, UK: Cambridge University Press, 1968).

18. John B. Stewart, *The Moral and Political Philosophy of David Hume* (New York: Columbia University Press, 1963), pp. 105-96.

19. Quoted in Michael Perelman, *Classical Political Economy: Primitive Accumulation and the Social Division of Labor* (Totowa, NJ: Rowman and Allanheld, 1983), p. 87.

20. Adam Smith, *Lectures on Jurisprudence [1762-1763]*, edited by Ronald L. Meek, David D. Raphael, and Peter Stein (Oxford: Clarendon Press, 1978); see also Meek, *Social Science*, pp. 68-130.

21. J. Ralph Lindgren, *The Social Philosophy of Adam Smith* (The Hague: Martinus Nijhoff, 1973), pp. 63-81.

22. Anthony Pagden, "The 'Defence of Civilization' in Eighteenth-Century Social Theory," *History of the Human Sciences* 1, no. 1 (Spring 1988): 34.

23. Quoted by Lucien Febvre, "Civilisation: Evolution of a Word and a Group of Ideas," in Peter Burke, ed., *A New Kind of History from the Writings of Febvre* (New York: Harper and Row Publishers, 1973), pp. 222-24, 232-33.

24. Febvre, ibid., pp. 240-47.

25. Eric Hobsbawm, *The Age of Revolution, 1789—1848* (New York: Mentor Books, 1962), pp. 202-17.

26. Alan Swingewood, *A Short History of Sociological Thought* (New York: St. Martin's Press, 1984), pp. 36-40.

27. Göran Therborn, *Science, Class and Society: On the Formation of Sociology and Historical Materialism* (London: New Left Books, 1976), pp.

145-219; Herbert Marcuse, *Reason and Revolution: Hegel and the Rise of Social Theory* (Boston: Beacon Press, 1960), pp. 323-60.

28. Kenneth E. Bock, "The Acceptance of Histories: Toward a Perspective for Social Science," *The University of California Publications in Sociology and Social Institutions* 3, no. 1 (1956): 5.

29. Eric J. Hobsbawm, *The Age of Capital, 1848—1875* (New York: Mentor Books, 1975); Richard Drinnon, *Facing West: The Metaphysics of Indian-Hating and Empire-Building* (New York: Mentor Books, 1980); and Reginald Horsman, *Race and Manifest Destiny: The Origins of American Racial Anglo-Saxonism* (Cambridge, MA: Harvard University Press, 1981).

30. John Burrow, *Evolution and Society: A Study in Victorian Social Theory* (Cambridge, UK: Cambridge University Press, 1970); Robert E. Bieder, *Science Encounters the Indian, 1820-1880: The Early Years of American Ethnology* (Norman: University of Oklahoma Press, 1986); Paul Q. Hirst, *Social Evolution and Sociological Categories* (London: George Allen and Unwin, 1976).

31. Lewis Henry Morgan, *Ancient Society, or, Researches in the Lines of Human Progress from Savagery Through Barbarism to Civilization* (Cleveland: Meridian Books, 1963), pp. 537, 561.

32. Donald M. Nonini, "Varieties of Materialism," *Dialectical Anthropology* 10 no. 1-4 (June 1985): 10-14; see also Herbert Spencer, *Social Statics: Or, The Conditions Essential to Human Happiness Specified, and The First of Them Developed* (London: Chapman, 1851) and "Progress: Its Law and Cause," *Essays: Scientific, Political, and Speculative* (London: Williams and Norgate, 1901) 1, pp. 8-62.

33. Robert Young, "Malthus and the Evolutionists: The Common Context of Biological and Social Theory," *Past and Present*, no. 143 (1969): 109-45; see also Greta Jones, *Social Darwinism and English Thought: The Interaction Between Biological and Social Theory* (Brighton, UK: Harvester, 1980); Richard Hofstadter, *Social Darwinism in American Thought* (Boston: Beacon Press, 1992).

34. Charles Darwin, *The Descent of Man and Selection in Relation to Sex* (London: Murray, 1874), p. 142.

35. Quoted by Horsman, *Race and Manifest Destiny*, p. 226.

36. Quoted by Allan Chase, *The Legacy of Malthus: The Social Costs of the New Scientific Racism* (Urbana: University of Illinois Press, 1980), p. 8.

37. John Bodnar, *Remaking America: Public Commemoration and Patriotism in the Twentieth Century* (Princeton, NJ: Princeton University Press, 1992), p. 30; see also Robert W. Rydell, *All the World's a Fair: Visions of Empire at American International Expositions, 1876—1916* (Chicago: University of Chicago Press, 1984); Ronald Rainger, *An Agenda for Antiquity: Henry Fairfield Osborn and Vertebrate Paleontology at the*

American Museum of Natural History, 1890—1935 (Tuscaloosa: University of Alabama Press, 1991); and Anne McClintock, *Imperial Leather: Race, Gender and Sexuality in the Colonial Contest* (London: Routledge, 1995).

38. Quoted in Eric F. Goldman, *The Crucial Decade and After: America, 1945—1960* (New York, NY: Random House, 1960), pp. 59-61; see also David Green, *The Language of Politics in America: Shaping Political Consciousness from McKinley to Reagan* (Ithaca, NY: Cornell University Press, 1987), pp. 164-206.

39. David W. Noble, *The End of American History: Democracy, Capitalism, and the Metaphor of Two Worlds in Anglo-American Historical Writing, 1880—1980* (Minneapolis: University of Minnesota Press, 1985), pp. 3-15.

40. Karl Wittfogel, *Oriental Despotism: A Comparative Study of Total Power* (New Haven, CT: Yale University Press, 1957); see also Edward W. Said, *Orientalism* (New York: Vintage Books, 1978).

41. Julian H. Steward, "Area Research: Theory and Practice," *Social Science Research Council Bulletin* 63 (New York, 1950): 102-105.

42. Piotr Sztompka, *The Sociology of Social Change* (Oxford: Blackwell Publishers, 1994), pp. 129-41; P.W. Preston, *Theories of Development* (London: Routledge and Kegan Paul, 1982), p. 58.

43. Sztompka, ibid., pp. 69-86, 129-41.

44. Richard Slotkin, *Gunfighter Nation: The Myth of the Frontier in Twentieth-Century America* (New York: Atheneum, 1992), p. 648; H. Bruce Franklin, *M.I.A. or Mythmaking in America* (Brooklyn, NY: Lawrence Hill Books, 1992); Samuel P. Huntington, *The Clash of Civilizations? The Debate* (New York: Council on Foreign Relations, 1993); see also chapter 1.

CHAPTER 3: CIVILIZATION AND ITS CRITICS

1. Thomas C. Patterson, "Early Colonial Encounters and Identities in the Caribbean: A Review of Some Recent Works and Their Implications," *Dialectical Anthropology* 16 (1991), no. 1: 1-14.

2. Lesley B. Simpson, *The Encomienda in New Spain: The Beginning of Spanish Mexico* (Berkeley: University of California Press, 1966), pp. xiii, 8, 176.

3. Juan Friede and Benjamin Keen, eds., *Bartolomé de las Casas in History: Toward an Understanding of the Man and His Work* (DeKalb: Northern Illinois University Press, 1971); and Benjamin Keen, *The Aztec Image in Western Thought* (New Brunswick, NJ: Rutgers University Press, 1971), pp. 70-99; Simpson, *The Encomienda in New Spain*, pp. 123-144.

4. Anthony Pagden, "Dispossessing the Barbarian: The Language of Spanish Thomism and the Debate over the Property Rights of the American Indians," in Padgen, ed., *The Languages of Political Theory in Early-Modern Europe* (Cambridge, UK: Cambridge University Press, 1987), pp. 89-94.

5. Juan Friede, "Las Casas and Indigenism in the Sixteenth Century," in Friede and Keen, *Bartolomé de las Casas in History*, p. 180; Pagden, ed., *The Languages of Political Theory*, pp. 67-75.

6. David B. Quinn, "Ireland and Sixteenth Century European Expansion," *Historical Studies* 1 (1958): 24-27; and "Sir Thomas Smith (1513—1577) and the Beginnings of English Colonial Theory," *Proceedings of the American Philosophical Society* 89 (1945) no. 4: 545-547.

7. V. Afanasiev, "The Literary Heritage of Bartolomé de Las Casas," in Friede and Keen, *Bartolomé de las Casas in History*, pp. 555-63; see also Geoffrey Parker, *The Dutch Revolt* (Ithaca, NY: Cornell University Press, 1977).

8. Peter Burke, *Popular Culture in Early Modern Europe* (New York: Harper and Row, 1978), pp. 260-61; Parker, *The Dutch Revolt*, pp. 109-10, 121-35, 148-49.

9. V.G. Kiernan, *State and Society in Europe, 1550—1650* (Oxford: Basil Blackwell, 1980), pp. 83-97; Perez Zagorin, *Rebels and Rulers, 1500—1660*, vol. 2 (Cambridge, UK: Cambridge University Press, 1982), pp. 51-86.

10. Josephine Diamond, "Montaigne's 'Des Cannibales': Savage Society and Wild Writing," in Christine W. Gailey, ed., *Dialectical Anthropology: Essays in Honor of Stanley Diamond*, vol. 1 (Gainesville: Flordia University Presses, 1992), pp. 42-43; Michel de Montaigne, *The Complete Essays of Montaigne*, translated by Donald M. Frame (Stanford, CA: Stanford University Press, 1965), pp. v-xiv.

11. Diamond, "Montaigne's 'Des Cannibales,' " pp. 38-39.

12. Montaigne, *The Complete Essays*, p. 505.

13. Ibid., p. 153.

14. Ibid., p. 155.

15. Ibid., p. 159.

16. Christopher Hill, *The World Turned Upside Down: Radical Ideas during the English Revolution* (Harmondsworth, UK: Penguin Books, 1975), p. 122. See also David W. Petegorsky, *Left-Wing Democracy in the English Civil War: A Study of the Social Philosophy of Gerrard Winstanley* (New York: Haskell House Publishers, 1972); and George M. Shulman, *Radical and Reverence: The Political Thought of Gerrard Winstanley* (Berkeley: University of California Press, 1989); and Timothy Kenyon, *Utopian Communism and Political Thought in Early Modern England* (London: Pinter Publishers, 1989).

17. Kenyon, ibid., p. 131.
18. Hill, *The World Turned Upside Down*, pp. 132-33.
19. Petegorsky, *Left-Wing Democracy*, p. 144.
20. Ibid.
21. Ibid., p. 189.
22. Ibid., p. 192.
23. Shulman, *Radical and Reverence*, pp. 103-15. Christopher Hill's *The English Bible and the Seventeenth-Century Revolution* (Harmondsworth, UK: Penguin Books, 1994) outlines the importance of the Bible and the political uses to which it was put. For a discussion of the prophetic tradition and its significance, both historically and today, see Michel Clévenot, *Materialist Approaches to the Bible* (Maryknoll, NY: Orbis Books, 1985) and Walter Brueggemann, *The Prophetic Imagination* (Philadelphia: Fortress Press, 1978).
24. Anthony Pagden, "The 'Defence of Civilization' in Eighteenth-Century Social Theory," *History of the Human Sciences* 1, no. 1 (Spring 1988): 34.
25. Maurice Cranston, *Jean-Jacques: The Early Life and Work of Jean-Jacques Rousseau, 1712—1754* (New York: W.W. Norton and Company, 1983), p. 272.
26. Jean Jacques Rousseau, *A Discourse on the Arts and Sciences* in *The Social Contract and the Discourses*, translated by G.D.H. Cole (London: J.M. Dent, 1973), p. 16.
27. Ibid., pp. 4-6.
28. Rousseau quoted in Cranston, *Jean-Jacques*, p. 243.
29. Jean Jacques Rousseau, *A Discourse on the Origin of Inequality* in Cranston, ibid., p. 89.
30. Ibid., p. 104.
31. Frederick M. Barnard, *Herder's Social and Political Thought* (Oxford: Clarendon Press, 1965), p. 118. This section follows the arguments of Gyorgy Markus, "Culture: The Making and the Make-up of a Concept (An Essay in Historical Semantics)," *Dialectical Anthropology* 18, no. 1 (1993): 3-29, and Raymond Williams, *Keywords: A Vocabulary of Culture and Society* (New York: Oxford University Press, 1983), pp. 87-93; in Paul Edwards, ed., *The Encyclopedia of Philosophy* (New York: Macmillan and The Free Press, 1967), 2nd ed., s.v. "Culture and Civilization," pp. 273-76, and *Culture and Society: 1780—1950* (New York: Columbia University Press, 1983).
32. Robert J.C. Young, *Colonial Desire: Hybridity in Theory, Culture and Race* (London: Routledge, 1995), pp. 36-43.
33. Frederick C. Beiser, *Enlightenment, Revolution, and Romanticism: The Genesis of Modern German Political Thought, 1790—1800* (Cambridge, MA: Harvard University Press, 1992), pp. 215-16, 189-221; see also Barnard, *Herder's Social and Political Thought*, pp. 139-41.

34. Beiser, ibid., pp. 206-207.
35. Ibid., pp. 76-77.
36. Barnard, *Herder's Social and Political Thought*, p. 77.
37. Ibid., p. 79.
38. Ibid., p. 80.
39. Ibid., p. 82.
40. Beiser, *Enlightenment, Revolution, and Romanticism*, pp. 213-14; Barnard, ibid., pp. 65-66; Clévenot, *Materialist Approaches*, pp. 1-41. See also Robert B. Coote and Mary P. Coote, "Power, Politics, and the Making of the Bible," in Norman Gottwald and Richard A. Horsley, eds., *The Bible and Liberation: Political and Social Hermeneutics* (Maryknoll, N.Y.: Orbis Books, 1993), pp. 343-64.
41. Samuel Taylor Coleridge, "On the Constitution of Church and State," *Collected Works*, vol. 10, (Princeton, NJ: Princeton University Press, 1976), pp. 42-43, 48-49.
42. Karl Marx and Frederick Engels, *Manifesto of the Communist Party* [1848], in *Selected Works in One Volume* (New York: International Publishers, 1968), pp. 39-40.
43. Lawrence Krader, ed., *The Ethnological Notebooks of Karl Marx* [1880—1882] (Assen, The Netherlands: Van Gorcum and Company, 1974); Frederick Engels, *The Origin of the Family, Private Property and the State* [1884], edited by Eleanor B. Leacock (New York: International Publishers, 1972).
44. Engels, *The Origin of the Family*, p. 233.
45. Ibid., p. 161.
46. Ibid., p. 232.
47. Ibid., p. 235.
48. Christine W. Gailey, "Community and State in Marx's *Ethnological Notebooks*" (Paper presented at the annual meeting of the Canadian Ethnology Society, Toronto, May 1985), p. 9.
49. John Stuart Mill, *Dissertations and Discussions Political, Philosophical, and Historical* (New York: Haskell House Publishers, 1973) 1, pp. 399-400.
50. Walter Rauschenbusch, *Christianity and the Social Crisis* (Louisville, KY: Westminster/John Knox Press, 1991), pp. 279-84.
51. John R. Pottenger, *The Political Theory of Liberation Theology: Toward a Reconvergence of Social Values and Social Science* (Albany: State University of New York Press, 1989).
52. Sigmund Freud, *Civilization and Its Discontents* (New York: W. W. Norton and Company, 1961), p. 88. This section builds on John Laffey, *Civilization and Its Discontented* (Montreal: Black Rose Books, 1993), especially pp. 101-52.

53. Freud, ibid., p. 59.
54. Sigmund Freud, *Future of an Illusion* (New York: W. W. Norton and Company, 1961), pp. 2-3.
55. Ibid., p. 4.
56. Ibid., pp. 5-6.
57. Ibid., p. 15.
58. Ibid., pp. 4-5.
59. Freud, *Civilization and Its Discontents*, p. 42.
60. Ibid.
61. Robert J. Ackerman, *Nietzsche: A Frenzied Look* (Amherst: University of Massachusetts Press, 1990), pp. 32-33, 183; see also Mark Warren, *Nietzsche and Political Thought* (Cambridge, MA: The MIT Press, 1988), pp. 46-79; and Tracy B. Strong, *Friedrich Nietzsche and The Politics of Transfiguration* (Berkeley: University of California Press, 1988).
62. Cornel West, "The New Cultural Politics of Difference," in Russell Ferguson, Martha Gever, Trinh T. Minh-ha, and Cornel West, eds., *Out There: Marginalization and Contemporary Cultures* (Cambridge, MA: The MIT Press, 1990), pp. 19-35; Stuart Hall, "What is This 'Black' in Black Popular Culture?" in Gina Dent, ed., *Black Popular Culture: A Project by Michelle Wallace* (Seattle, WA: Bay Press, 1992), pp. 21-33.
63. See the various commentaries in Ashley Montagu, ed., *Toynbee and History: Critical Essays and Reviews* (Boston: Porter Sargent Publisher, 1956).

CHAPTER 4: INVENTING BARBARIANS AND OTHER UNCIVILIZED PEOPLES

1. Stanley Diamond, *In Search of the Primitive: A Critique of Civilization* (New Brunswick, NJ: Transaction Books, 1974), p. 1.
2. Michel Clévenot, *Materialist Approaches to the Bible* (Maryknoll, NY: Orbis Books, 1985), pp. 1-41; Robert B. Coote and Mary P. Coote, "Power, Politics, and the Making of the Bible," in Norman Gottwald and Richard A. Horsley, eds., *The Bible and Liberation: Political and Social Hermeneutics* (Maryknoll, NY: Orbis Books, 1993), pp. 343-364.
3. Christopher Hill, *The English Bible and the Seventeenth-Century Revolution* (Harmondsworth, UK: Penguin Books, 1994), p. 5.
4. Tony Bennett, "Texts in History: The Determination of Readings and Their Texts," in Derek Attridge, Geoff Bennington, and Robert Young, eds., *Post-Structuralism and the Question of History* (Cambridge, UK: Cambridge University Press, 1987), pp. 70-71.
5. Raymond Williams, "Ideas of Nature," in his *Problems in Materialism*

and Culture: Selected Essays (London: Verso, 1980), p. 67; for further discussion, see R.G. Collingwood, The Idea of Nature (London: Oxford University Press, 1960); Clarence J. Glacken, Traces on the Rhodian Shore: Nature and Culture in Western Thought from Ancient Times to the End of the Eighteenth Century (Berkeley: University of California Press, 1967); C.S. Lewis, Studies in Words (Cambridge, UK: Cambridge University Press, 1960), pp. 24-74; Max Oelschlaeger, The Idea of Wilderness (New Haven, CT: Yale University Press, 1991); Alexander Wilson, The Culture of Nature: North American Landscape from Disney to the Exxon Valdez (Cambridge, MA: Blackwell, 1992).

6. Williams, Problems in Materialism and Culture, p. 68.

7. Edith Hall, Inventing the Barbarian: Greek Self-Definition through Tragedy (Oxford: Clarendon Press, 1991); Moses I. Finley, The World of Odysseus (London: Penguin Books, 1979); see also Thomas C. Patterson, Archaeology: The Historical Development of Civilizations (Englewood Cliffs, NJ: Prentice-Hall, 1993), pp. 199-201, 216-18, 232-39.

8. Thucydides, History of the Peloponnesian War (Harmondsworth, UK: Penguin Books, 1972), p. 38; see also H.C. Baldry, The Unity of Mankind in Greek Thought (Cambridge, UK: At the University Press, 1965), pp. 12-15.

9. Raphael Sealey, A History of the Greek City States, 700-338 B.C. (Berkeley: University of California Press, 1976), pp. 169-231; G.E.M. de Ste. Croix, The Class Struggle in the Ancient Greek World (Ithaca, NY: Cornell University Press, 1981), pp. 278-326; Roger Stritmatter, "Oedipus, Akhnaton and the Greek State: An Archaeology of the Oedipus Complex," Dialectical Anthropology 12 (1987), pp. 45-64.

10. Hall, Inventing the Barbarian, pp. 6-15, 80, 146, 201, 214.

11. Helen H. Bacon, Barbarians in Greek Tragedy (New Haven, CT: Yale University Press, 1961), and Timothy Long, Barbarians in Greek Comedy (Carbondale: Southern Illinois University Press, 1986).

12. Hall, Inventing the Barbarian, pp. 201-13; Arlene W. Saxonhouse, Fear of Diversity: The Birth of Political Science in Ancient Greek Thought (Chicago: University of Chicago Press, 1992), pp. 77-78.

13. Stritmatter, "Oedipus, Akhnaton and the Greek State," pp. 50-51; Froma I. Zeitlin, "The Dynamics of Misogyny: Myth and Mythmaking in the Oresteia," Arethusa 11 (1978), no. 1-2, pp. 149-55; Page duBois, Centaurs and Amazons: Women and the Pre-History of the Great Chain of Being (Ann Arbor: University of Michigan Press, 1982), pp. 110-28.

14. Hall, Inventing the Barbarian, pp. 213-21.

15. Ellen Meiksins Wood, Peasant-Citizen and Slave: The Foundations of Athenian Democracy (London: Verso, 1988), pp. 142-46; see also Ellen Meiksins Wood and Neal Wood, Class Ideology and Ancient Political

Theory: Socrates, Plato, and Aristotle in Social Context (Oxford: Basil Blackwell, 1978).

16. Mary R. Lefkowitz, *Women in Greek Myth* (Baltimore: Johns Hopkins University Press, 1986), pp. 112-13; Patricia Springborg, *Western Republicanism and the Oriental Prince* (Austin: University of Texas Press, 1992), pp. 23-40; Brent D. Shaw, " 'Eaters of Flesh, Drinkers of Milk': The Ancient Mediterranean Ideology of the Pastoral Nomad," *Ancient Society* 13/14 (1982/1983), pp. 18-20.

17. W.R. Jones, "The Image of the Barbarian in Medieval Europe," *Comparative Studies in Society and History* 13, no. 4 (1971): 397.

18. Ibid., p. 376-81; Roger Bartra, *Wild Men in the Looking Glass: The Mythic Origins of European Otherness* (Ann Arbor: University of Michigan Press, 1994); and A.N. Sherwin-White, *Racial Prejudice in Imperial Rome* (Cambridge, UK: At the University Press, 1970); Sarah B. Pomeroy, *Goddesses, Whores, Wives, and Slaves: Women in Classical Antiquity* (New York: Schocken Books, 1975).

19. Janet Abu-Lughod, *Before European Hegemony: The World System A.D. 1250—1350* (Oxford: Oxford University Press, 1989); Agnes Heller, *Renaissance Man* (New York: Schocken Books, 1978).

20. Ibn Khaldn, *The Muqaddimah: An Introduction to History*, edited by N.J. Dawood (Princeton, NJ: Princeton University Press, 1967).

21. John H. Rowe, "The Renaissance Foundation of Anthropology," *American Anthropologist* 67 (1965):1-20; Roberto Weiss, *The Renaissance Discovery of Classical Antiquity* (Oxford: Basil Blackwell, 1988).

22. Jones, "The Image of the Barbarian in Medieval Europe," pp. 387-404; and Richard Bernheimer, *Wild Men in the Middle Ages: A Study in Art, Sentiment, and Demonology* (Cambridge, MA: Harvard University Press, 1952), pp. 9-12.

23. Quoted in Jones, ibid., p. 396.

24. Thomas C. Patterson, "Early Colonial Encounters and Identities in the Caribbean: A Review of Some Recent Works and Their Implications," *Dialectical Anthropology* 16 (1991), no. 1: 1-14.

25. Ibid.

26. Lewis Hanke, *Aristotle and the American Indians: A Study in Race Prejudice in the Modern World* (Bloomington: Indiana University Press, 1959).

27. Karen Spalding, *Huarochirí: An Andean Society under Inca and Colonial Rule* (Stanford, CA: Stanford University Press, 1984).

28. James Lockhart, *Spanish Peru, 1532—1560: A Colonial Society* (Madison: University of Wisconsin Press, 1968), pp. 133-49; Karen Spalding, "Social Climbers: Changing Patterns of Mobility among the Indians of Colonial Peru," *Hispanic American Historical Review* 50 (1970): 646-64.

29. Quoted by Karen Spalding, "Social Stratification and Colonial Revolt," manuscript, p. 31.

30. Juan Carlos Estenssoro, "Modernismo, estética, música y fiesta: elites y cambio de actitud frente a la cultura popular. Perú, 1750—1850," manuscript; Jalil Sued Badillo, "The Theme of the Indigenous in the National Projects of the Hispanic Caribbean," in Peter Schmidt and Thomas C. Patterson, eds., *Writing Alternative Histories* (Santa Fe, NM: SAR Press, 1995).

31. William Robertson, *The History of America* (London: Printed for A. Strahan, 1778), vol. 1, pp. 308-14, 324-40, 410-11; vol. 2, pp. 268-99, 323.

32. Quoted in George Rudé, *The Crowd in History, 1730—1848* (New York: John Wiley and Sons, 1964), p. 8.

33. Robert A. Nye, *The Origins of Crowd Psychology: Gustave LeBon and the Crisis of Mass Democracy in the Third Republic* (London: Sage Publications, 1975), pp. 33-34, 50.

34. Ibid., p. 67.

35. Richard Slotkin, *The Fatal Environment: The Myth of the Frontier in the Age of Industrialization, 1800—1890* (Middletown, CT: Wesleyan University Press, 1985), pp. 480-81.

36. Daniel Pick, *Faces of Degeneration: A European Disorder, c. 1848—c. 1918* (Cambridge, UK: Cambridge University Press, 1989), pp. 109-54; Robert J. C. Young, *Colonial Desire: Hybridity in Theory, Culture and Race* (London: Routledge, 1995), pp. 55-118; Sander L. Gilman, *Difference and Pathology: Stereotypes of Sexuality, Race, and Madness* (Ithaca, NY: Cornell University Press, 1985); J. Edward Chamberlain and Sander Gilman, *Degeneration: The Dark Side of Progress* (New York: Columbia University Press, 1985); and Anne McClintock, *Imperial Leather: Race Gender and Sexuality in the Colonial Contest* (London: Routledge, 1995).

37. Quoted by Allan Chase, *The Legacy of Malthus: The Social Costs of the New Scientific Racism* (Urbana: University of Illinois Press, 1980), p. 186.

38. Jon Beckwith and Jonathan King, "The XYY Syndrome: A Dangerous Myth," in the Science for the People Genetics and Social Policy Study Groups, *I.Q. Scientific or Social Controversy?* (February 1976), pp. 39-43. See also William H. Tucker, *The Science and Politics of Racial Research* (Urbana: University of Illinois Press, 1994); Stefan Kühl, *The Nazi Connection: Eugenics, American Racism, and German National Socialism* (Oxford, UK: Oxford University Press, 1994); and Paul Weindling, *Health, Race and German Politics Between National Unification and Nazism, 1870—1945* (Cambridge, UK: Cambridge University Press, 1989).

39. Christine W. Gailey, "Evolutionary Perspectives on Gender Hierarchy," in Beth B. Hess and Myra M. Ferree, eds., *Analyzing Gender: A Handbook*

of Social Science Research (Beverly Hills, CA: Sage Publications, 1988), pp. 32-67; Carole Pateman, *The Disorder of Women* (Stanford, CA: Stanford University Press, 1989), pp. 1-16.

40. Londa Schiebinger, *Nature's Body: Gender and the Making of Modern Science* (Boston: Beacon Press, 1993), pp. 143, 175-79.

41. Thomas Laqueur, *Making Sex: Body and Gender from the Greeks to Freud* (Cambridge, MA: Harvard University Press, 1990).

42. Schiebinger, *Nature's Body*, pp. 53, 147-48; Carole Pateman, *The Disorder of Women* and *The Sexual Contract* (Stanford, CA: Stanford University Press, 1988).

43. Laqueur, *Making Sex*, pp. 199-201.

44. Ibid., pp. 114-92.

45. Terrence W. Epperson, "The Politics of Empiricism and the Construction of Race as an Analytical Category," *Transforming Anthropology* 5 (1994), nos. 1-2: 16.

46. Ibid.

47. Thomas C. Patterson and Frank Spencer, "Racial Hierarchies and Buffer Races," *Transforming Anthropology* 5 (1994), nos. 1-2: 20.

48. Ibid: 20-21.

49. Richard Drinnon, *Facing West: The Metaphysics of Indian-Hating and Empire-Building* (New York: New American Library, 1980); Reginald Horsman, *Race and Manifest Destiny: The Origins of American Racial Anglo-Saxonism* (Cambridge, MA: Harvard University Press, 1981).

50. Stephen Jay Gould, *The Mismeasure of Man* (New York: W.W. Norton, 1981), pp. 30-72, and *Ontology and Phylogeny* (Cambridge, MA: Harvard University Press, 1977), pp. 120-46.

51. John S. Haller, Jr., *Outcasts from Evolution: Scientific Attitudes of Racial Inferiority, 1859-1900* (Urbana: University of Illinois Press, 1971), pp. 60-68, 147-48; Patterson and Spencer, "Racial Hierarchies and Buffer Races," p. 22.

52. Horsman, *Race and Manifest Destiny*, pp. 182-83; 226.

53. Patterson and Spencer, "Racial Hierarchies and Buffer Races," p. 22.

54. Karen Brodkin Sacks, "How Did Jews Become White Folks?" in Steven Gregory and Roger Sanjek, eds., *Race* (New Brunswick, NJ: Rutgers University Press, 1994), pp. 78-102; Noel Ignatiev, *How the Irish Became White* (New York: Routledge, 1995).

55. Allen Chase, *The Legacy of Malthus: The Social Costs of the New Scientific Racism* (Urbana: University of Illinois Press, 1980); Elazar Barkan, *The Retreat of Scientific Racism: Changing Conceptions of Race in Britain and the United States between the World Wars* (Cambridge, UK: Cambridge University Press, 1992), pp. 62-134.

56. Garland E. Allen, "The Misuse of Biological Hierarchies: The American

Eugenics Movement, 1900—1940," *History and Philosophy of the Life Sciences* 5(2) (1983), pp. 105-28.
57. Sacks, "How Did Jews Become White Folks?" For a discussion of the effects this had in the academy, see Thomas C. Patterson, *Toward a Social History of Archaeology in the United States* (Ft. Worth, TX: Harcourt Brace College Publishers, 1995), pp. 80-83, 107-108.
58. UNESCO, *The Race Concept: The Result of an Inquiry* (Paris: UNESCO, 1952); M.F. Ashley Montagu, *Man's Most Dangerous Myth: The Fallacy of Race* (New York: Columbia University Press, 1942) and *The Idea of Race* (Lincoln: University of Nebraska Press, 1965).
59. Nathan Glazer and Daniel P. Moynihan, *Beyond the Melting Pot* (Cambridge, MA: MIT Press, 1983).
60. Herrnstein and Murray, *The Bell Curve*; and Dinesh D. D'Souza, *The End of Racism* (New York: The Free Press, 1995).

CHAPTER 5: UNCIVILIZED PEOPLES SPEAK

1. Jalil Sued Badillo, "The Theme of the Indigenous in the National Projects of the Hispanic Caribbean," in Schmidt and Patterson, eds., *Making Alternative Histories*; Richard Price, ed., *Maroon Societies: Rebel Slave Communities in the Americas* (Baltimore: Johns Hopkins University Press, 1979); Gerald M. Sider, *Lumbee Indian Histories: Race, Ethnicity and Indian Identity in the Southern United States* (Cambridge, UK: Cambridge University Press, 1993).
2. Karen Brodkin Sacks, personal communication; see also her "How Did Jews Become White Folks?" in Gregory and Sanjek, eds., *Race*, pp. 78-102.
3. Georg W.F. Hegel, *The Phenomenology of Mind* (London: George Allen and Unwin, 1966), pp. 235-37; Jean Jacques Rousseau, *The Social Contract and Discourses* (London: J.M. Dent and Sons, 1973), pp. 168-75; Friedrich Nietzsche, *Beyond Good and Evil* (Harmondsworth, UK: Penguin Books, 1973) and *On the Genealogy of Morals* (New York: Vintage Books, 1967); Tracy B. Strong, *Friedrich Nietzsche and the Politics of Transfiguration* (Berkeley: University of California Press, 1988), pp. 237-59, 351- 53.
4. W.E.B. DuBois, *The Souls of Black Folk* [1903] (New York: New American Library, 1969), p. 204. See the illuminating discussions by Deborah K. King, "Multiple Jeopardy, Multiple Consciousness: The Context of Black Feminist Ideology," *Signs* 14(1) (1988): 42-72, and Ernest Allen, Jr., "Ever Feeling One's Twoness: 'Double Ideals' and 'Double Consciousness' in *The Souls of Black Folk,*" *Critique of Anthropology* 12(3) (1992): 261-276.

5. DuBois, *The Souls of Black Folk*, p. 45.
6. Ibid., p. 221.
7. Quoted in Mamie E. Locke, "From Three-Fifths to Zero: Implications of the Constitution for African-American Women, 1787—1870," in Darlene C. Hine, Wilma King, and Linda Reed, eds., *We Specialize in the Wholly Impossible: A Reader in Black Women's History* (Brooklyn, NY: Carlson Publishing, 1995), p. 226.
8. Young Joseph, "An Indian's View of Indian Affairs," *North American Review* 269 (1879):431-432.
9. Allan Bloom, *The Closing of the American Mind* (New York: Simon and Schuster, 1987); and Lynn Cheney, *Humanities in America: A Report to the President, the Congress, and the American People* (Washington, DC: National Endowment for the Humanities, 1988). For the social and political context of the attack, see Michael Bérubé and Cary Nelson, eds., *Higher Education under Fire: Politics, Economics, and the Crisis of the Humanities* (New York: Routledge, 1995); John K. Wilson, *The Myth of Political Correctness: The Conservative Attack on Higher Education* (Durham, NC: Duke University Press, 1995), Cornel West, *Beyond Eurocentrism and Multiculturalism*, 2 vols. (Monroe, ME: Common Courage Press, 1993), Paul Berman, *Debating P.C.: The Controversy over Political Correctness on College Campuses* (New York: Dell Publishing, 1992) and David Theo Goldberg, ed., *Multiculturalism: A Critical Reader* (Cambridge, MA: Basil Blackwell, 1994).
10. Herrnstein and Murray, *The Bell Curve* and Fraser, ed., *The Bell Curve Wars*.
11. Angelo Falcón, "Puerto Rican and the Politics of Racial Identity," in Herbert W. Harris, Howard C. Blue, and Ezra E.H. Griffith, eds., *Racial and Ethnic Identity: Psychological Development and Creative Expression* (New York: Routledge, 1995), pp. 197-98; see also Clara Rodríguez, "Challenging Racial Hegemony: Puerto Ricans in the United States," in Gregory and Sanjek, eds., *Race*, pp. 131-45.
12. Dwight Conquergood, "For the Nation! How Street Gangs Problematize Patriotism," in Herbert W. Simons and Michael Billig, eds., *After Postmodernism: Reconstructing Ideology Critique* (Beverly Hills, CA: Sage Publications, 1994), p. 205.
13. See the essays in Sandra Harding, ed., *The "Racial" Economy of Science: Toward a Democratic Future* (Bloomington: Indiana University Press, 1993).
14. Gail Bederman, " 'Civilization,' The Decline of Middle-Class Manliness, and Ida B. Wells's Antilynching Campaign (1892—1894)," in Hine, King, and Reed, eds., *We Specialized in the Wholly Impossible*, pp. 407-32.

15. Ibid., p. 424.
16. Christine W. Gailey, *From Kinship to Kingship: Gender Hierarchy and State Formation in the Tongan Islands* (Austin: University of Texas Press, 1987), p. 6.
17. Quoted in Meredith Tax, *The Rising of the Women* (New York: Monthly Review Press, 1980), p. 230.
18. Quoted in Suzanne Lebsock, "Woman Suffrage and White Supremacy: A Virginia Case Study," in Nancy A. Hewitt and Suzanne Lebsock, eds., *Visible Women: New Essays on American Activism* (Urbana: University of Illinois Press, 1993), p. 62.
19. Quoted in Locke, "From Three-Fifths to Zero," p. 232.
20. Deborah G. White, "The Cost of Club Work, The Price of Black Feminism," in Hewitt and Lebsock, eds., *Visible Women*, p. 258.
21. Ibid., p. 258.
22. Ibid., p. 251.
23. Ibid.
24. Ibid., pp. 259-64.
25. Lebsock, "Woman Suffrage and White Supremacy," p. 81.
26. Tera W. Hunter, "Domination and Resistance: The Politics of Wage Household Labor in New South Atlanta," in Hine, King, and Reed, eds., *We Specialized in the Wholly Impossible*, p. 352.
27. Rosalyn Baxendall and Linda Gordon, *America's Working Women: A Documentary History, 1600 to the Present* (New York: W.W. Norton and Company, 1995), p. 236.
28. Ibid., pp. 236-37.
29. Cornel West, *Race Matters* (Boston: Beacon Press, 1993), p. 52.
30. Ibid., pp. 53-54.

INDEX